Vintage Knits for Modern Babies

VINTAGE KNITS
for Modern Babies

Hadley Fierlinger

PHOTOGRAPHY BY ANGELA LANG

TEN SPEED PRESS

Berkeley

Ten Speed Press and the Ten Speed Press colophon are
registered trademarks of Random House, Inc.

Illustrations on pages 13, 14, 15, and 83 by Tannya Harricks.
Used with permission.

The blossom pattern on page 66, © Nicky Epstein, is reprinted
from *Nicky Epstien's Knitted Flowers* with permission from the author
and Sixth&Spring Books.

Library of Congress Cataloging-in-Publication Data
Fierlinger, Hadley.
   Vintage knits for modern babies / Hadley Fierlinger.
      p. cm.
   Includes index.
   Summary: "A collection of 25 knitting patterns for baby and toddler clothing
and accessories, based on vintage designs"—Provided by publisher.
   ISBN-13: 978-1-58008-960-9
   ISBN-10: 1-58008-960-7
1. Knitting—Patterns. 2. Infants' clothing. 3. Infants' supplies. I. Title.
   TT825.F554 2009
   746.43'2041—dc22
                                        2009008446

ISBN 978-1-58008-960-9

Printed in China

Design by Katy Brown

10 9 8 7 6 5 4 3 2 1

First Edition

For Grammy and Marion, who are forever in my heart

Contents

Acknowledgments

· ·

This book was made possible by the people close to me and some who are very far away.

First I would like to thank good friend Heidi Swanson, who made the book a possibility, along with Julie Bennett at Ten Speed Press, who helped me form the idea. Thank you to my wonderful editor, Brie Mazurek, who made the process easy and stress free. Thanks also to designer Katy Brown for these beautiful pages.

I have a great deal of thanks to my mom and dad, who have supported everything I have done and helped me grow into who I am today.

Deepest thanks to Jo Reeve, my savior, who kindly helped me with pattern making when I was stuck.

Many thanks to Pauline the knitter, who deserves her name on the cover for quickly knitting everything in this book (and much more).

Thanks to my Wellington stitch-n-bitch posse; Lesleigh, Kristy, Merryn, Sally, Tannya, Virginia, and Wanda. A special thank you to the amazing seamstress Lesleigh, who made some of the dresses that appear in the photographs.

Thanks to Angela Lang and her family for her beautiful photographs. I would also like to thank the child models and their families: Aidan Mogal, Josh Mogal, and Katy Haberkern; Camila; Camille, Rebecca, and Victor Amato; Griffen; Madhavi Kennedy, Craig Kennedy, and Urmila Raghavan; Milan, Wonny, and Joe Mullen; Rowan, Alana, and Zach Thompson; Simon, Kristen, and Jim Policy; and Ella, Julie, and Rodney Walker.

Thank you to Tannya Harricks, who did the illustrations in the book and has always been my partner in crime when it comes to project ideas and inspiration.

Finally, and most important, I am the luckiest woman alive to spend every day of my life with three of the most gorgeous boys I have ever known; thanks Philip, Emory, and Jasper for supporting all my work and letting me have my time and space to be a girl in a house of boys.

Introduction

. . . .

Most of us knit for babies today because we want to, not because we have to. We knit for them, as our grandmothers did, for the love of it. We knit because nothing else can give us the same soothing texture and emotion as a garment created by hand. While we sit and knit, our hopes and dreams are wrapped in every stitch.

Few things are more scrumptious than the cozy warmth of a new baby swaddled in a lovingly hand-knit blanket. We can practically smell the heavenly scent of that loved and worn blanket nestled under the chin of its tiny owner.

My passion for baby knits was born years ago when I met my friend's new baby, Anya. She was wearing a beautiful tiny white eyelet cardigan that had been expertly hand knit. When I asked Anya's mother where she bought it, she explained that her own grandmother had knit it for *her* back in the 1960s. She had worn it as a baby, and she had saved it for her future babies. The cardigan Anya wore was in perfect condition, not a stain or pulled thread, after all those years. Every time I saw Anya after that, she wore a different vintage cardigan layered over a simple white T-shirt, just as her mother had more than thirty years earlier. It is a timeless style that captures the simplicity of babyhood—cozy, comfortable, practical, and sweet.

Inspired by Anya's sweaters, I promised myself that I would learn to knit, so one day I could create my own beautiful heirlooms for my children and grandchildren. With my newfound knitting passion, I launched Shescraftyknits.com in 2002, selling my own designs of hand knit baby wear. Over the years, I have designed knitting patterns that capture vintage style and meet modern necessity—less-complicated, updated classics that hark back to simpler days.

Heirlooms from Generations Past

Many of us have a baby keepsake box in which our mothers kept treasured mementos from our first year. If there was a knitter in your family, your keepsake box most likely contains a pair of tiny booties recording the brief moment when your feet were no bigger than a doll's. Perhaps you recall poking your toes through the holes of an afghan that always adorned the family sofa. These family heirlooms are treasures created to give warmth to the wearer and tactile memories that last a lifetime. If you are lucky, you may have a whole box of baby knits lovingly saved to pass down to your own children and grandchildren so you can continue the tradition.

Generations ago, knitting was an important skill that every girl needed to learn from an early age. In the beginning of the twentieth century, no shops sold layettes (complete outfits for newborn infants) or diapers, and knitters in the family had to create *everything* a baby was going to need for the first year (and beyond). Before published knitting patterns became available, knitters used jotted-down "recipes" with guides on the general shape and size of a garment to be knit. The recipes were shared within the family and community to create practical garments such as socks, underwear, stockings, and baby clothes. Families knew the importance of thrift as well as the practicality of wool, which was the primary knitting yarn.

Early knitting pattern books started to appear in the late 1800s and were filled with very sensible everyday items for the whole family. In the early 1900s few women could afford to buy a ready-made baby layette, which was only available to the very wealthy, so everything was knit at home. To prepare for a new baby, most mothers created layette items months in advance. A lucky family would have an aunt or a grandmother busily knitting to help fill baby's clothes drawers with fancy dresses, gowns, coats, and frilly bonnets for outings and celebrations. Babies mostly required simple items such as wool soakers, rompers, vests, blankets, leggings, and plenty of caps and booties. The most popular knitting patterns were designed with simplicity and thrift in mind. Usually they were made on very skinny needles with thin baby yarn, which took quite a while to knit and produced very delicate garments.

As babies grew, their fashions became more detailed. A few key items became the essentials that every toddler needed in the wardrobe: sturdy woolen pullovers for busy boys, fine merino twin sets for little girls, lacy eyelet cardigans for wearing with skirts, classic coats for wearing over baby's Sunday best, angora jackets to put on over a dress, and spiffy berets and caps to accessorize outfits. After being worn by the current baby, these well-made garments would be carefully boxed up and saved for later children in the family to wear. The best patterns and designs would be kept in the family and used over and over for new nieces, nephews, and grandchildren, becoming family heirlooms.

Knitting for Modern Babies

The popularity of knitting ebbed and flowed during the twentieth century, becoming especially strong during economic recessions. In hard times, people

"I sat down and started knitting and realized quickly that I didn't need the pattern after all. I knew it. I'm not sure I could have written it out, but as my hands were moving and the booties were growing, I knew what came next. It made me smile—thinking of my Meme and her knitted blankets—always one in a basket by her sofa for the latest cousin to be born; my Nana and her stash of baby sweaters—always a few in progress, always a few in a pile waiting for one baby or another; my mother with her crocheted baby blankets. Not all of these women were heavy knitters or crocheters, but still they had their baby 'thing' that they made, and gave, and *knew by heart*. My mind wandered to the massive imaginary pile of hand knits—piles of love—made by all these women before me, and [the piles] I have yet to knit, and those that will be knit in years to come by little ones now. And all the love and hope that gets knit into each and every one."

—AMANDA BLAKE SOULE, BLOGGER (WWW.SOULEMAMA.COM)
AND AUTHOR OF *THE CREATIVE FAMILY*

turned to knitting because they could make things that they could not afford to buy.

The last decade has seen a return to the craft of hand knitting with emphasis on the activity rather than the product. Today's modern yarns appeal to young urban knitters who desire fashionable color palettes and luxurious fibers. Modern knitters have rediscovered the craft of hand knitting because it is fun, social, creative, and satisfying to make stylish garments that cannot be bought in stores. Knitting blogs and social networking sites like Ravelry.com have driven this new age of knitting, giving like-minded knitters a place to swap, sell, and share patterns, techniques, and inspiration.

We no longer need to knit baby's entire wardrobe for the sake of frugality, but babies still need a selection of practical favorites and some elegant pieces for special occasions. Today, even if you are short on time, you can knit something to mark the precious time when a baby is small. Infants need many simple caps and booties to help keep them warm, so a new mother always appreciates the gift of these hand knit pieces. If you start an heirloom blanket at the news of a pregnancy, you'll have plenty of time to complete all those long rows.

Like many people, you may have a favorite item that you make when you learn that a baby is on the way. Often it's a pattern that is quick and easy to knit using your favorite yarn. Knitting it over and over becomes so enjoyable and routine that you may no longer need to look at the pattern. Before you know it, you've created a basket of booties ready to give as last-minute gifts. What better way to welcome a little one into the world than with a gift made by hand?

Choosing Yarns for Baby Knits

Modern babies need not suffer the itchy torture of the hand knit woolen sweaters we were forced to endure as children. Today, we are lucky to have so many soft, gorgeous yarn options. Our grandmothers were not as lucky as we are. During wartime, finding yarn for a needed garment often meant unraveling old sweaters and knitting something new with the tangled, bumpy mess.

During the 1950s, less-expensive modern fibers such as nylon, orlon, and courtelle were an obvious

"My grandmother would gather us kids around and try to maintain her patience to teach us to knit. I would sort of get the hang of it, but my grandmother was so good at it I would sometimes get discouraged. I especially felt like I would never learn when I watched my grandmother fall asleep in her recliner with her knitting needles in her hands . . . still knitting. Yes, my grandmother could knit asleep (or at least lying back with her eyes closed, snoring)."

—HEATHER BROSSMAN, MOTHER OF THREE

choice, because they were easy to machine-wash, and they dried quickly. The new yarns created a tremendous demand for new patterns and knitting books. Women's monthly magazines often included knitting patterns, many of them for babies and children.

When our grandmothers needed wool for their stash, they could run down to the local five-and-dime. Every department store also had a well-stocked yarn department, and much of the yarn was either synthetics or the coarse wool that some of us remember being forced to wear as kids. Sixty years ago, baby yarn was very limited in color, unlike the rainbow selection today.

Knitters now have almost too many choices when it comes to yarn. From bamboo to silk, cashmere to cotton, we are overwhelmed with selection. As mothers and grandmothers from around the world know, when knitting for babies there is no better yarn than wool, because animal fibers like wool and alpaca are excellent insulators while allowing the skin to breathe and stay dry. Air circulation prevents germs from growing, making wool an antibacterial material. Because of these unique properties, wool was used as a cover for cloth diapers. It is also naturally flame retardant and will not ignite, which makes it especially safe for baby bedding and sleepwear. Wool can be worn in winter as well as during the cool nights of summer, because of its superior temperature-regulating properties.

There is a new awareness that natural fibers are far better for baby as well as the environment. Modern yarns made from natural fibers, such as organically grown cotton, wool, and bamboo, are popular in this age of allergies, asthma, and skin sensitivities. Modern eco yarns not only are a smart choice for the environment but also can be sourced locally and from independent producers in a wide variety of beautiful styles. Many home spinners sell small batches of hand-dyed yarns that are truly works of art. I have not specified any of these yarns in my patterns simply because they are not easily available to most readers; however, I encourage you to substitute suitable yarns in my patterns when you can (see Materials).

New and beautiful plant-based yarns are now made from bamboo, hemp, soy, and flax. I find that these fibers are best blended with animal fibers or cotton for baby knits, because the mixture seems to enhance their drape, insulation properties, and loft. For babies I prefer 100% merino wool or a blend of fibers, such as the Debbie Bliss and Rowan yarns that combine merino wool, cashmere, and microfiber. This mixed yarn can produce a strong, durable garment that holds its shape, is easy to care for, and is exceptionally soft—perfect for little ones!

Here are some common yarns and blends I use in this book:

- **Wool:** The natural fiber spun from the fleece of sheep. It is durable, is elastic, and has excellent insulating properties. Merino wool comes from merino sheep and is considered the finest wool yarn because of its longer fibers.

- **Alpaca:** The natural fiber spun from the hair of an alpaca. It is silky, soft, durable, and luxurious. While similar to sheep's wool, it is much warmer and has none of the prickly feel of wool. Garments knit with alpaca are lightweight and incredibly warm, ideal for baby. Alpaca is commonly blended with wool to increase its elasticity and maximize its uses.

- **Angora:** The natural, hollow-chambered hair from Angora rabbits, heavenly soft, fine, and many times warmer than sheep's wool. It provides the best natural insulation, while allowing body moisture to escape, keeping the wearer warm and dry. Pure angora can be too fluffy for baby knits, so I recommend a blended yarn like Angora Merino from Sublime, a blend of extra-fine merino wool with angora.

- **Cotton:** A relatively lightweight plant fiber that is good for summer clothing and blankets. It is quite breathable and is comfortable to wear next to the skin. Blue Sky Organic cotton is grown and harvested without agrichemicals and is exceptionally soft and lovely for baby garments. Cotton does not have the elasticity of wool, and some find it difficult to knit for this reason.

- **Cotton and Wool:** A blend such as Wool Cotton by Rowan is extremely soft next to delicate skin yet strong and luxurious. The 50% wool gives the yarn more elasticity and warmth than cotton alone would have. This yarn has a lovely texture and drape.

- **Cashmere:** Made from the underhair of the cashmere goat and known for its luxurious softness. Combined with merino wool and microfiber, as in Cashmerino yarns from Debbie Bliss and Cashsoft by Rowan, it is a delightful yarn for babies.

- **Silk and Cashmere:** An exquisite blend of silk with the best-quality Himalayan cashmere fiber. This noble yarn has an extraordinary softness on the skin.

For the patterns in this book, I have, wherever possible, chosen yarns that are easy to care for and lovely to knit with. Most of the yarns wear well and, with proper care, make great heirlooms for future owners. The suppliers are listed at the end of the book, in case your local yarn shop does not carry a particular one. In many patterns you can easily substitute a yarn of comparable weight if you are careful to do a gauge square before starting, to ensure perfect results.

Garment Care

Always follow the care instructions on the yarn label, as each fiber has its own requirements. I have chosen yarns that are hand washable or machine washable wherever possible, for ease of care.

Washing and drying knits: If the yarn specifies hand washing, use a tiny bit of wool detergent (I love Ecover and Soak). Hand knits should never be rubbed with soap; instead, gently move them around in the water. Rinse in clean water, remove in a bundle without twisting, wrap in a towel, and gently squeeze out the water. Never hang a knitted garment to dry, as hanging destroys the shape. Air-dry on a flat surface on top of a clean cloth or towel. Keep out of direct sun, as the rays can yellow some light fibers. Dry cleaning is not recommended, because the residual chemicals can harden the fabric.

Storing: To preserve your heirloom knits undamaged for future generations, it is important to store them properly. First wash and press the garment, and wrap it in acid-free tissue paper (available at packaging stores). Then seal it in an airtight plastic storage container or zippered freezer bag to protect it for years and keep moths out.

Mothballs are no longer considered safe to use, because they contain harmful chemicals. Many natural remedies help repel moths. One of the most popular ingredients that our grandmothers used is lavender, which can often be found in moth-repelling wash products for wool items. Or knit the easy Lavender Sachet (page 79) to store with your knits or to give as a gift. Other popular herbs that are thought to repel moths include rosemary, mint, thyme, ginseng, cloves, and lemon. Regularly check your

"We were sitting on a bench in front of my grandmother's house, and my dear mother cast on the stitches and tried to teach me how to knit. I have been knitting my entire life. I'm now seventy-two. Every so often my memory goes back to sitting on that bench in Baltimore with my dear mother wearing a 1940s-style cotton housedress, her sweet face looking down at me, and trying like hell to get my fingers moving."

—SANDY WAYNE TUBMAN, SHESCRAFTY CUSTOMER

stored garments to refresh the herbs and see that each garment is safe.

About the Patterns

I created this pattern book to share with you some of my favorite classic knits for babies. While several patterns are for the beginning knitter, most cater to those who have mastered the basics and whose skills include basic shaping and following intermediate instructions.

Many of the designs were inspired by my growing collection of vintage knitting pattern books, which date back to the 1890s. I also included well-loved patterns from my Shescraftyknits.com collection, such as the Double-Breasted Car Coat, Matinee Jacket, and Cabled Booties, as well as Anya's Cardigan, which inspired me so many years ago. You'll find simple yet timeless designs that are waiting for your own modern touch and embellishment. Have fun adding vintage buttons, simple embroidery, playful pom-poms, and fabric-covered buttons to your creations. I hope you find many inspirations in this book. Happy knitting!

"My grandmother . . . made us amazing aaron [cabled] and bobbled jackets, dress/ knicker/bonnet/bootie sets for our dolls, pom-pom hats, etc. I was first shown how to knit by Mum's mother; she was Danish, so I was taught the Danish way (holding the wool in the left hand, not the right) and was watched with much curiosity by other school friends and their mothers when I 'knitted funny.' I liked knitting a lot and was very patient with it; my knit rows were always very tight, and purl very loose, but after a year or so I realized that my other grandmother knitted the 'normal' way, and she seemed to go much faster, so I spent hours on the couch next to her when they visited, copying her and eventually taught myself to knit in the normal style—with much better results!"

—CATHERINE WALKER, AVID KNITTER

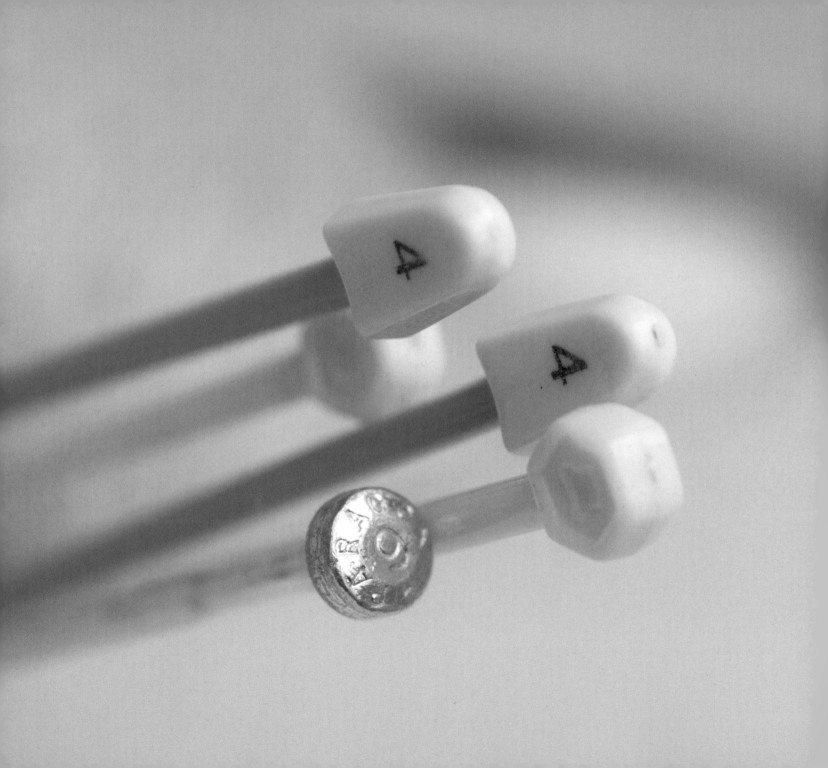

Pattern Instructions & Special Techniques

. . . .

*"In through the front door, once
around the back, peek through the
window, and off jumps Jack."*

*"Into the bunny hole, run around the tree,
out of the bunny hole, away runs he."*

*"Under the fence, catch the sheep,
back you go, off you leap."*

There are many rhymes to help teach children to knit—you may remember one of your own from childhood. Most of the patterns in this book assume a basic knowledge of knitting techniques. If you are new to knitting, it pays to have a great instructional book or website handy that can help you along the way (see Resources on page 88 for suggestions).

Always read a knitting pattern through before beginning to knit. You will understand more about the construction of the garment and the plan to get you to the goal.

Pattern Skill Level

For each pattern, I indicate a skill level:

- **Beginner:** Suitable for a novice knitter who is familiar with reading a pattern and abbreviations, and who can cast on, knit, purl, bind off, and work very basic shaping.

- **Intermediate:** Suitable for a knitter with more than beginner experience in increasing, decreasing, shaping, and basic knitting terminology.

- **Experienced:** Suitable for the knitter who is well versed in lace, shaping, yokes, and more complicated pattern work.

Sizes

Instructions for each pattern are given for a first size, with larger sizes in parentheses. The patterns are for ages from zero months to three years. If you are in doubt about which size to knit, it is always better to choose the larger size, because baby can grow into the garment or wear it earlier with the sleeves rolled up or with socks on under the booties.

Materials

Each pattern has a list of the materials you will need: kind and amount of yarn, size of knitting needles, stitch markers, buttons, and so on. If you wish to substitute other yarns, I urge you to first check your gauge, as described next.

Gauge

At the start of each pattern, the required knitting gauge is given. Before you begin, it is very important to check your gauge by knitting a gauge square. Using the yarn, needle size, and stitch pattern specified, cast on 40 stitches, and work approximately 40 rows. Lay your work flat and, without stretching, measure 4 inches (10 cm) both vertically and horizontally, marking the measure with pins. Count the stitches between pin markers; these should match the required gauge. If not, try one needle size up or down: if your gauge is too loose (too few stitches and rows), try smaller needles; if it is too tight (too many stitches and rows), try larger needles. Incorrect gauge will produce a misshapen project and lots of tears!

Special Techniques

Here are directions for some techniques and embellishments that I use in several of the patterns.

Cloth-Covered Buttons

Creating your own little buttons using your favorite vintage fabric adds a special touch to your finished garment. They are easy to make and endless in their possibilities. Put them on booties, use them on cardigans, or add them as little decorations to items such as the Baby Clothes Hanger Covers (page 58).

You need a cloth-covered button set from your favorite craft shop (I prefer the metal buttons) and your favorite fabric. Each button set varies in its instructions, so follow the ones on the package.

Knitting Motifs (Duplicate Stitch)

Duplicate stitch is a great way to add a motif or a bit of color to your knitted garment. I love the fact that I don't have to play around with intarsia or complicated instructions while I am knitting—I can add my designs after I finish (or not). Duplicate stitch is especially handy to cover a stain on a baby's sweater. Because the stitches lie on top of the V of the stocking stitch, it looks like it is part of the original knitting.

It is a good idea to plan where your embroidery is going to go, keeping in mind that the motif is created on the front side of stocking stitch. To make a duplicate stitch, use the same weight yarn as for the garment. From the back of the garment, insert a threaded yarn needle through the base of the stitch you're duplicating (no need to make a knot, but do leave a tail to weave in later). Pass the needle from right to left behind the stitch directly above. Insert needle back through the starting point. Repeat for each stitch.

Work across the design from the right top (or bottom, if you prefer) to the left, moving up, down, or to the left as needed. When you come to the end of a row, turn the work upside down, and work the next row from right to left also.

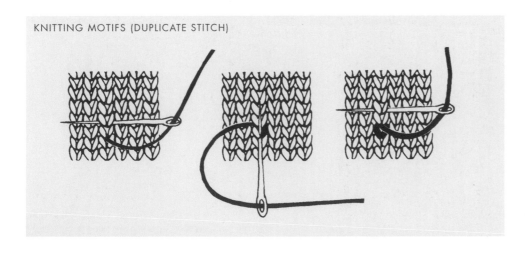

KNITTING MOTIFS (DUPLICATE STITCH)

Twisted Cord

Twisted cord is very easy to make and can be used as a durable tie, trim, or decorative element in your projects. You make it by twisting strands of yarn together. Cut a length of yarn 3 times the length of cord you want, fold it in half, and tie the ends together with a knot about 1 inch (2.5 cm) from the end. I use a clothespin to secure one end of the doubled yarn to a firm object and then pull the yarn taut and begin to twist it in one direction until it is tightly twisted. Keeping the strands taut, fold the piece of yarn in half, and allow the strands to twist around each other. Tie a knot at the unknotted end to secure.

Pom-Poms

Pom-poms are easy to make and add a vintage element to the tops of caps and hoods or the ends of cords.

To make them, cut 2 circular pieces of cardboard the width of the desired pom-pom (cereal boxes are a good source of cardboard), and cut a center hole in each. Holding the two circles together, insert your yarn needle and desired yarn through the hole and around the outside of the cardboard many times, working around the circle. When you can't fit the needle through the hole any longer you are finished.

Pull the two cardboard circles apart, and cut the yarn between them around the circle. Tie a length of yarn tightly around the strands between the two circles. Remove the cardboard, and trim the pom-pom to size.

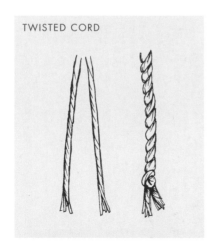

TWISTED CORD

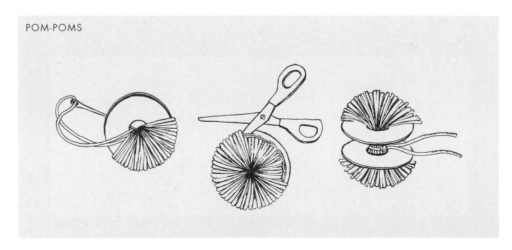

POM-POMS

Lazy Daisy

The lazy daisy is a very old, classic embroidery stitch that can be added to almost any knit garment easily.

You need a long strand of yarn, a yarn needle, and some knit fabric in need of embellishing. Thread the needle, and tie a knot at the end of the yarn. Decide where you want the center of your flower to be, and bring the needle up through that spot, from back to front, pulling the yarn all the way through.

Put the needle back through the work in exactly the same spot from front to back. Pull the yarn through slowly, and when the loop that's left on the front is the size you want your flower petal to be, bring the needle back up through the work where you want the end of the petal to be. Make a short stitch there over the petal yarn to tack it in place.

Bring the needle back to the center and repeat for each of the 5 petals. Knot the yarn in back when finished.

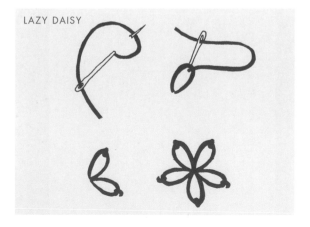
LAZY DAISY

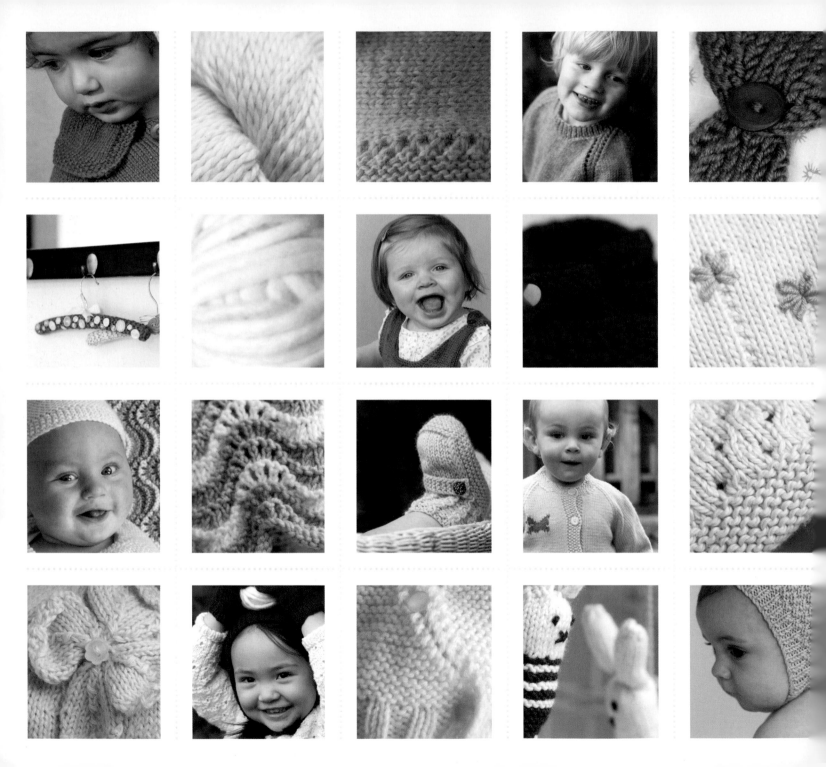

The Patterns

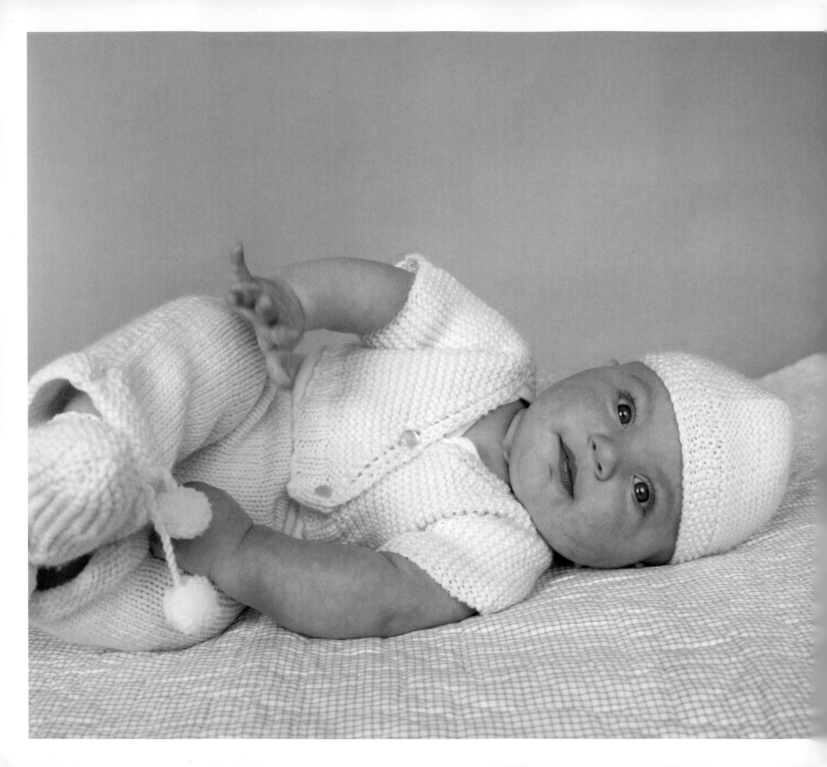

Layette Cap

Babies need so many caps during their first few months, to help regulate their body temperature. This simple cap is easy to knit with seed and garter stitches. It's made with a gorgeous merino blend that is machine washable for easy care. You could easily substitute a soft cotton for warmer climates.

Sizes

0–3 (3–6, 6–12) months

Finished Measurements

Circumference: 12" (13", 14") (30.5 [33, 36] cm)

Materials

1 (1, 1) 50 g ball RYC Cashsoft Baby DK (57% extra-fine merino, 33% microfiber, 10% cashmere; 143 yds [130 m]), in #801 Horseradish

US 6 (4 mm) straight needles

Yarn needle for finishing

Gauge

22 sts and 28 rows make 4" (10 cm) in garter st

Directions

Cap

CO 61 (71, 81) sts.

Rows 1–8: K1, *p1, k1; rep from * to end.

Change to garter st (knit all sts each row), and work until hat measures 3" (3½", 4") (8 [9, 10] cm) from beg.

Crown Shaping

Row 1: K1, *k2tog, k8; rep from * to end—55 (64, 73) sts.

Row 2 and all even rows: Knit.

Row 3: K1, *k2tog, k7; rep from * to end—49 (57, 65) sts.

Row 5: K1, *k2tog, k6; rep from * to end—43 (50, 57) sts.

Row 7: K1, *k2tog, k5; rep from * to end—37 (43, 49) sts.

Cont to dec in this manner on every other row, working 1 fewer st between decs each time, until 13 (15, 17) sts rem.

Next row: K1, *k2tog; rep from * to end—7 (8, 9) sts.

Finishing

Break off yarn, and thread it through rem sts. Pull tight, and secure end. Join seam. Weave in ends.

Pom-Pom Booties

Every baby needs a few pairs of wool booties to keep little toes warm and snug during the first year before shoes are needed. These easy-to-knit booties stay on kicking little feet with the help of tiny pom-pom ties. After baby has grown out of them, save them in a memory box for the child to see how tiny his or her feet once were.

Sizes

0–3 (3–6, 6–12) months

Materials

1 (1, 1) 50 g ball RYC Cashsoft Baby DK (57% extra-fine merino, 33% microfiber, 10% cashmere; 143 yds [130 m]) in #801 Horseradish

US 3 (3.25 mm) straight needles

US 6 (4 mm) straight needles

2 twisted cords (see page 14) 12" (30 cm) long

4 (1" [2.5 cm]) pom-poms (see page 14)

Needle and thread to match yarn

Gauge

22 sts and 28 rows make 4" (10 cm) on larger needles in garter st

Directions

Bootie (Make 2)

Begin at center of sole.

On larger needles, CO 27 (33, 39) sts.

Row 1 and all odd rows: Knit.

Row 2: K1, *inc1, k10 (13, 16), inc1; rep from * once—31 (37, 43) sts.

Row 4: K1, *inc1, k12 (15, 18), inc1, k1; rep from * once—35 (41, 47) sts.

Row 6: K1, *inc1, k14 (17, 20), inc1; rep from * once—39 (45, 51) sts.

Row 8: K1, *inc1, k16 (19, 22), inc1, k1; rep from * once—43 (49, 55) sts.

Knit 5 (7, 9) rows.

Instep Shaping

Row 1: K24 (28, 30), k2tog tbl, turn.

Row 2: (K1, p1) 2 (3, 3) times, k1, p2tog, turn.

Row 3: (P1, k1) 2 (3, 3) times, p1, k2tog tbl, turn.

Row 4: (K1, p1) 2 (3, 3) times, k1, p2tog, turn.

Repeat Rows 3–4 until 31 (33, 37) sts rem.

Next row: (P1, k1) 2 (3, 3) times, p1, k2tog tbl, knit to end—30 (32, 36) sts.

Change to smaller needles.

Knit 2 rows.

Next row (eyelet row): K2, *yo, k2tog; rep from * to end.

Knit 15 (17, 17) rows.

BO.

Finishing

Join back, heel, and sole seam. Thread twisted cord through eyelets of each bootie, and sew pom-poms to ends of cords.

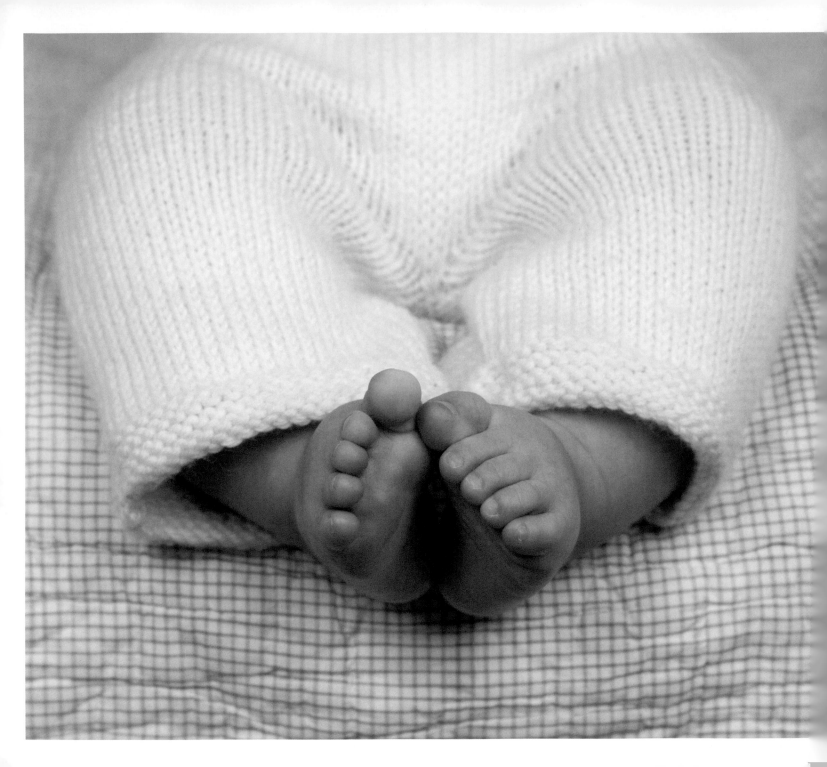

Tiny Trousers

Keeping baby's lower half warm can sometimes be a challenge, but not so with these cozy little stocking stitch pants with a garter stitch hem. They knit up in no time. The elastic thread is sewn into the ribbed waist to make changes quick. Knit with easy-care yarn, the trousers can be machine- or hand-washed to keep them looking spiffy.

Sizes

0–3 (3–6, 6–12) months

Finished Measurements

Waist: 18½" (20½", 22") (47 [52, 56] cm)

Length: 12½" (14½", 16½") (32 [37, 42] cm)

Materials

3 (3, 4) 50 g balls RYC Cashsoft Baby DK (57% extra-fine merino, 33% microfiber, 10% cashmere; 143 yds [130 m]) in #801 Horseradish

US 3 (3.25 mm) straight needles

US 6 (4 mm) straight needles

Stitch holder

Yarn needle for finishing

2 (24" [60 cm]) elastic threads for waist

Gauge

22 sts and 30 rows make 4" (10 cm) on larger needles in St st

Directions

Back/Front (Make 2)

❀ *First Leg*

On larger needles, CO 26 (29, 31) sts. Knit 8 rows garter st, inc 2 sts evenly across last row—28 (31, 33) sts.

Cont in St st until work measures 5½" (7", 9") (14 [18, 22] cm) from beg, ending with a purl row.**

Sl sts onto stitch holder.

❀ *Second Leg*

Work same as first leg to **.

Leave sts on needle.

Crotch and Trunk

Row 1 (RS): K26 (29, 31) sts of second leg, k2tog, sl sts from stitch holder onto left needle, sl1, k1, psso, knit to end—54 (60, 64) sts.

Work even until work measures 11½" (13½", 15½") (29 [34, 39] cm) from beg, ending with a knit row.

Next row (WS): Purl, dec 3 sts evenly across—51 (57, 61) sts.

Waistband

Change to smaller needles.

Row 1 (RS): K2, *p1, k1; rep from * to last st, k1.

Row 2 (WS): P2, *k1, p1; rep from * to last st, p1.

Rep Rows 1–2 twice more (6 rows rib in all).

BO loosely in rib.

Finishing

Join side and leg seams using mattress stitch. Thread 2 rows of elastic thread through WS of rib at waistline. Weave in yarn ends.

Crossover Jacket

BEGINNER / INTERMEDIATE

Quickly knit in garter stitch, this darling cropped crossover jacket is the perfect little layer for newborns. It is a great pattern for beginning knitters who are looking for something a little more challenging, using simple shaping and easy eyelet edging that doubles as buttonholes.

Sizes

0–3 (3–6, 6–12) months

Finished Measurements

Chest width: 18" (20", 22") (46, [51, 56] cm)

Length from back neck: 6" (6½", 7") (15 [16.5, 18] cm)

Materials

2 (2, 3) 50 g balls RYC Cashsoft Baby DK (57% extra-fine merino, 33% micro-fiber, 10% cashmere; 143 yds [130 m]) in #801 Horseradish

US 6 (4 mm) straight needles

Stitch holder

Yarn needle for joining seams and attaching buttons

2 (½" [13 mm]) shank buttons

Gauge

22 sts and 28 rows make 4" (10 cm) in garter st

Directions

Right Front

CO 34 (38, 42) sts.

Row 1 (RS): K2, *p2, k2; rep to end.

Row 2 (WS): P2, *k2, p2; rep to end.

These 2 rows form rib pattern. Rep Rows 1–2 until work measures 1" (2.5 cm), ending on Row 2 (WS).

Change to garter st and cont as follows:

Row 1 (RS): K2, yo, k2tog, knit to end.

Row 2 (WS): K to last 5 sts, k2tog, k3—1 st dec'd.

Rep Rows 1–2 until work measures 2¼" (2½", 3") (5.5 [6.5, 7.5] cm) from beg, ending with a RS row.

Next row (WS): CO 10 sts, k to last 5 sts, k2tog, k3—9 sts added.

Rep Rows 1–2 until 19 (22, 25) sts rem. Work even until work measures 6" (6½", 7") (15 [16.5, 18] cm) from beg, ending with a WS row (Row 2). Sl sts to a stitch holder. Break yarn, and set piece aside while you work left front.

Left Front

CO 34 (38, 42) sts, and work k2, p2 rib as for right front.

Change to garter st and cont as follows:

Row 1 (RS): K to last 4 sts, k2tog, yo, k2.

Row 2 (WS): K3, k2tog, knit to end—1 st dec'd.

Rep Rows 1–2 until work measures 2¼" (2½", 3") (5.5 [6.5, 7.5] cm) from beg, ending with a WS row (Row 2).

Next row (RS): CO 10 sts, k to last 4 sts, k2tog, yo, k2—9 sts added.

Next row (WS): Work same as Row 2.

Rep Rows 1–2 until 19 (22, 25) sts rem. Work even until work measures 6" (6½", 7") (15 [16.5, 18] cm) from beg, ending with a WS row (Row 2).

Leave sts on needle.

Back

Continuing with shoulder stitches of left front on needle, with RS facing, k19 (22, 25) sts. Then CO 24 sts, and pick up and k19 (22, 25) sts of right front shoulder from stitch holder. These 62 (68, 74) sts are for back, which you'll knit from top to bottom.

Knit all rows until work measures 10" (10¼", 10½") from beg.

BO off 10 sts at beg of next 2 rows. Knit even until work measures 11" (11½", 12") (28 [29, 30.5] cm) from beg, ending with a WS row and dec 1 st at each end of last row—40 (46, 52) sts.

Work in k2, p2 rib for 1" (2.5 cm). BO in rib.

Finishing

Join side seams and underarm seams. Sew on buttons evenly spaced on left front, using holes in eyelet edging for buttonholes.

Matinee Jacket

EXPERIENCED

This darling little jacket with a simple seed stitch yoke is ideal for special outings. Using a cashmere/merino/microfiber blend, the jacket is extremely soft and warm yet machine washable for practicality.

Sizes

3–6 (6–12, 12–24) months

Finished Measurements

Chest width (buttoned): 21½" (23½", 24½") (54.5 [59.5, 62] cm)

Length from back neck: 10½" (11", 14") (26.5 [28, 35.5] cm)

Sleeve seam: 5" (6", 7") (12.5 [15, 17.5] cm)

Materials

3 (4, 4) 50 g balls Debbie Bliss Cashmerino DK (55% merino wool, 33% microfiber, 12% cashmere; 125 yds [114 m]) in #04 Red

US 3 (3.25 mm) straight needles

US 6 (4 mm) straight needles

US 6 (4 mm) 24" (60 cm) circular needle

5 stitch holders

Yarn needle for finishing and attaching buttons

2 (½" [13 mm]) shank buttons

Gauge

22 sts and 28 rows make 4" (10 cm) on larger needles in St st

Directions

Back

On smaller needles, CO 55 (61, 65) sts.

Rows 1–8: K1, *p1, k1; rep from * to end.

Change to larger needles, and cont in St st, beg with a knit row, until work measures 6" (7", 8") (15 [17.5, 20] cm) from beg, ending with a WS row. Sl sts onto a stitch holder.

Left Front

On smaller needles, CO 35 (37, 39) sts.

Rows 1–8: K1, *p1, k1; rep from * to end.

Change to larger needles.

Row 9 (RS): K to last 5 sts, work in seed st to end.

Row 10 (WS): Seed st 5, purl to end.

Rep Rows 9–10 until work measures 6" (7", 8") (15 [17.5, 20] cm) from beg, ending with a WS row. Sl sts onto a stitch holder.

Right Front

On smaller needles, CO 35 (37, 39) sts.

Rows 1–8: K1, *p1, k1; rep from * to end.

Change to larger needles.

Row 9 (RS): Seed st 5, knit to end.

Row 10 (WS): P to last 5 sts, seed st to end.

Rep Rows 9–10 until work measures 6" (7", 8") (15 [17.5, 20] cm) from beg, ending with a WS row. Sl sts onto a stitch holder.

Sleeve (Make 2)

On smaller needles, CO 33 (35, 37) sts.

Rows 1–6: K1, *p1, k1; rep from * to end.

(continued)

Rows 7–10: Change to larger needles. Work in St st, beg with a knit row.

Row 11: Inc1 st at each end of row and every 4th (4th, 6th) row foll, until you have 45 (47, 49) sts.

Work even until sleeve measures 5" (6", 7") (12.5 [15, 17.5] cm), ending with a WS row. Sl sts onto a stitch holder.

Yoke

With WS facing, sl sts from stitch holders onto circular needle in the foll order: left front, first sleeve, back, second sleeve, right front—215 (229, 241) sts.

Join yarn to right front edge with RS facing.

Row 1 (RS): Seed st 5, k to last 5 sts, seed st 5.

Row 2 (WS): Seed st 5, p to last 5 sts, seed st 5.

Row 3 (buttonhole): K1, p1, yo, p2tog, k to last 5 sts, seed st 5.

❀ *3–6 months:*

Row 4 (dec row): Seed st 5, *p4, p2tog; rep from * to last 6 sts, p1, seed st 5—181 sts.

Rows 5–9: Work even in seed st all across.

Row 10 (dec row): Seed st 5, *p3, p2tog; rep from * to last 6 sts, p1, seed st 5—147 sts.

Row 11: Seed st 5, k to last 5 sts, seed st 5.

Row 12: Seed st 5, p to last 5 sts, seed st 5.

Row 13: Seed st 5, k to last 5 sts, seed st 5.

Row 14 (dec row): Seed st 5, p2, *p3, p2tog; rep from * to last 10 sts, p5, seed st 5—121 sts.

Row 15 (buttonhole): K1, p1, yo, p2tog, work seed st to end.

Rows 16–19: Work in seed st.

Row 20 (dec row): Seed st 5, *p2, p2tog; rep from * to last 8 sts, p3, seed st 5—94 sts.

Row 21: Seed st 5, k to last 5 sts, seed st 5.

Row 22: Seed st 5, p to last 5 sts, seed st 5.

Row 23: Seed st 5, k to last 5 sts, seed st 5.

Row 24 (dec row): Seed st 5, *p2, p2tog; rep from * to last 5 sts, seed st 5—73 sts.

Rows 25–28: Work in seed st.

Row 29 (buttonhole): K1, p1, yo, p2tog, seed st to end.

Row 30 (dec row): Seed st 5, p1, *p1, p2tog; rep from * to last 7 sts, p2, seed st 5—53 sts.

Row 31: Purl.

Row 32: Knit.

BO loosely.

❀ *6–12 months:*

Row 4 (dec row): Seed st 5, p2, *p5, p2tog; rep from * to last 12 sts, p7, seed st 5—199 sts.

Rows 5–9: Work even in seed st all across.

Row 10 (dec row): Seed st 5, p2, *p5, p2tog; rep from * to last 10 sts, p5, seed st 5—173 sts.

Row 11: Seed st 5, k to last 5 sts, seed st 5.

Row 12: Seed st 5, p to last 5 sts, seed st 5.

Row 13: Seed st 5, k to last 5 sts, seed st 5.

Row 14 (dec row): Seed st 5, p2, *p4, p2tog; rep from * to last 10 sts, p5, seed st 5—147 sts.

Row 15–18: Work in seed st.

Row 19 (buttonhole): K1, p1, yo, p2tog, work in seed st to end.

Row 20 (dec row): Seed st 5, *p3, p2tog; rep from * to last 7 sts, p2, seed st 5—120 sts.

Row 21: Seed st 5, k to last 5 sts, seed st 5.

Row 22: Seed st 5, p to last 5 sts, seed st 5.

Row 23: Seed st 5, k to last 5 sts, seed st 5.

Row 24 (dec row): Seed st 5, p1, *p3, p2tog; rep from * to last 9 sts, p4, seed st 5—99 sts.

Rows 25–29: Work in seed st.

Row 30 (dec row): Seed st 5, *p2, p2tog; rep from * to last 6 sts, p1, seed st 5—77 sts.

Row 31: Seed st 5, k to last 5 sts, seed st 5.

Row 32: Seed st 5, p to last 5 sts, seed st 5.

Row 33 (buttonhole): K1, p1, yo, p2tog, k to last 5 sts, seed st 5.

Row 34 (dec row): Seed st 5, *p1, p2tog; rep from * to last 6 sts, p1, seed st 5—55 sts.

Row 35: Purl.

Row 36: Knit.

BO loosely.

❀ *12–24 months:*

Row 4 (dec row): Seed st 5, *p6, p2tog; rep from * to last 12 sts, p7, seed st 5—213 sts.

Rows 5–9: Work even in seed st all across.

Row 10 (dec row): Seed st 5, *p6, p2tog; rep from * to last 8 sts, p3, seed st 5—188 sts.

Row 11: Seed st 5, k to last 5 sts, seed st 5.

Row 12: Seed st 5, p to last 5 sts, seed st 5.

Row 13: Seed st 5, k to last 5 sts, seed st 5.

Row 14 (dec row): Seed st 5, *p5, p2tog; rep from * to last 8 sts, p3, seed st 5—163 sts.

Rows 15–19: Work in seed st.

Row 20 (dec row): Seed st 5, p1, *p5, p2tog; rep from * to last 10 sts, p5, seed st 5—142 sts.

Row 21 (buttonhole): K1, p1, yo, p2tog, k to last 5 sts, seed st 5.

Row 22: Seed st 5, p to last 5 sts, seed st 5.

Row 23: Seed st 5, knit to last 5 sts, seed st 5.

Row 24 (dec row): Seed st 5, p1, *p4, p2tog; rep from * to last 10 sts, p5, seed st 5—121 sts.

Rows 25–29: Work in seed st.

Row 30 (dec row): Seed st 5, *p3, p2tog; rep from * to last 6 sts, p1, seed st 5—99 sts.

Row 31: Seed st 5, k to last 5 sts, seed st 5.

Row 32: Seed st 5, p to last 5 sts, seed st 5.

Row 33: Seed st 5, k to last 5 sts, seed st 5.

Row 34 (dec row): Seed st 5, *p2, p2tog; rep from * to last 6 sts, p1, seed st 5—77 sts.

Rows 35–38: Work in seed st.

Row 39 (buttonhole): K1, p1, yo, p2tog, k1, seed st to end.

Row 40 (dec row): Seed st 5, *p1, p2tog; rep from * to last 6 sts, p1, seed st 5—55 sts.

Row 41: Purl.

Row 42: Knit.

BO loosely.

Finishing

Press lightly with warm iron and damp cloth. Join side and sleeve seams. Sew on 2 buttons opposite buttonholes. Weave in ends.

Ruby Slippers

These adorable bootie slippers with delicate shaping and a feminine strap make an elegant addition to a first wardrobe.

Sizes

3–6 (6–12) months

Materials

1 (1) 50 g ball Debbie Bliss Cashmerino DK (55% merino wool, 33% microfiber, 12% cashmere; 125 yds [114 m]) in #04 Red

US 7 (4.5 mm) straight needles

Yarn needle for finishing

2 (½" [13 mm]) shank buttons

Needle and thread to match yarn

Gauge

20 sts and 36 rows make 4" (10 cm) in garter st

Directions

Right Slipper

CO 32 (38) sts.

Row 1 (WS): Knit.

Row 2 (RS): K2, M1, k to last 2 sts, M1, k2—34 (40) sts.

Row 3: Knit.

Rep Rows 2–3 once—36 (42) sts.

Next row: K16 (19), (k1, M1) 4 times, knit to end—40 (46) sts.

Work even in garter st until shoe measures 1⅝" (4 cm) from beg, ending with a WS row.

Instep Shaping

Next row: K12 (15), (k2tog) 8 times, knit to end—32 (38) sts.

Next row: K22 (25), turn.

Next row: (K2tog) 6 times, k1, turn.

Next row: BO 8 sts loosely, knit to end—18 (24) sts.**

Strap

Next row: K9 (12), turn.

Next row: CO 8 (10) sts, knit to end.

Next row: K17 (22).

Next row (buttonhole): K1, k2tog, yo, knit to end.

BO 17 (22) sts purlwise.

Right Button Band

Knit 4 rows of rem 9 (12) sts.

BO purlwise.

Left Slipper

Work same as right slipper to **.

Left Button Band

K 4 rows of first 9 (12) sts on needle.

BO purlwise.

Strap

Rejoin yarn to rem 9 (12) sts on needle, CO 8 (10) sts, knit to end—17 (22) sts.

Knit 2 rows.

Next row (buttonhole): K to last 3 sts, yo, k2tog, k1.

BO purlwise.

Finishing

Join center back, heel, and sole seams. Weave in all ends. Sew on buttons.

Nana's Bunnies

BEGINNER / INTERMEDIATE

I borrowed this pattern from my friend Louise. For three generations, every newborn in her family has received one of Nana's Bunnies. When the children are old enough, they, too, are taught to knit these little heirlooms. After you knit a few, you will know the pattern without looking and be able to knit a great last-minute gift in a night. I have updated the pattern using cotton yarn with low-impact dyes, a safer choice than other yarns, because children are bound to suck on the bunnies.

Finished Measurements

Height: 5½"

Materials

1 65 g skein Blue Sky Alpacas Skinny Organic Cotton (100% cotton; 150 yds [137 m]) in #30 Birch (MC)

1 65 g skein Skinny Dyed Cotton in #305 Pink (CC)

US 4 (3.5 mm) straight needles

Yarn needle for finishing

Small amount of organic carded wool or polyester fiberfill or yarn scraps for stuffing

Yarn or embroidery thread and needle for embroidering on face and details

1 (¾" [2 cm]) pom-pom (see page 14)

Tip: The 2 skeins of yarn will make 2 to 3 bunnies, if you want to make several.

Gauge

28 sts and 34 rows make 4" (10 cm) in St st

Directions

Body

Beg at bottom of bunny. With MC, CO 12 sts.

Row 1: *Inc1; rep from * to end—24 sts.

Knit even for 7 more rows with MC.

Knit 8 rows with CC.

Knit 2 rows with MC.

Knit 2 rows with CC.

Knit 2 rows with MC.

Knit 2 rows with CC.

Next row: With MC, k4, (k2tog) twice, k8, (k2tog) twice, k4—20 sts.

Knit 1 row with MC.

Next row: With CC, k3, (k2tog) twice, k6, (k2tog) twice, k3—16 sts.

Knit 1 row with CC.

Break off CC.

Head

Cont on 16 sts in MC only.

Next row (RS): *K1, inc1; rep from * to end—24 sts.

Work 9 rows St st, ending with a purl row.

Next row: *K1, k2tog; rep from * to end—16 sts.

Next row: Purl.

Next row: *K2tog; rep from * to end—8 sts.

Using yarn needle, thread yarn through rem sts, pull tight, and fasten off, leaving a long tail for sewing up the back.

Ear (Make 2)

CO 6 sts with MC.

Row 1: *Inc1; rep from * to end—12 sts.

Work 11 rows in St st, ending with a purl row.

Next row: *K2tog; rep from * to end—6 sts.

BO.

Finishing

With RS together, using long yarn tail at top of head, sew back seam of head and body, leaving bottom open. Turn bunny right side out, stuff lightly, and then finish stitching bottom. To create "legs," using same yarn, stitch through stuffing up the middle about 1½" (4 cm) or to first band of CC. Join ear seam, stuff ears lightly, and sew to head. Weave in ends. Embroider face on bunny using embroidery thread or yarn oddments. Sew on pom-pom for the tail.

Bunny Mobile

INTERMEDIATE / EXPERIENCED

Using Nana's Bunnies, you can create this super-cute baby mobile to hang above a crib or changing table. Garter stitch chevrons make fun rickrack trim, and the soft colors and sweet bunny faces are sure to soothe fussy babies. Choose colors to complement the baby's room.

Finished Measurements

Length: 25½" (65 cm)

Materials

1 50 g ball Debbie Bliss Baby Cashmerino (55% merino, 33% microfiber, 12% cashmere; 137 yds [125 m]) in #700 Red

US 3 (3.25 mm) straight needles

7 (10" [25 cm]) lengths of twisted cord (see page 14)

8" (20 mm) wooden embroidery hoop (available at craft and sewing shops)

5 (1" [2.5 cm]) pom-poms (see page 14)

Needle and thread to match yarn

4 Nana's Bunnies (page 32), knit with Debbie Bliss Baby Cashmerino

2–4 clothespins

Yarn needle for finishing

Gauge

7 sts per 1 inch (2.5 cm)

Tip: To sl2, k1, psso, you slip 2 stitches to the right needle as if to knit them, knit the next stitch, and pass both slipped stitches over the knit one.

Directions

Rickrack Trim (Make 2)

CO 171 sts.

Row 1 (RS): K4, *sl2, k1, psso, k7; rep from * to last 7 sts, sl2, k1, psso, k4—137 sts.

Rows 2, 4, and 6: Knit.

Row 3: K1, *M1, k2, sl2, k1, psso, k2, M1 k1; rep from * to end.

Row 5: Rep Row 3.

Row 7: BO, working k1, *M1, k7, M1, k1; repeat from * across row.

Mobile Assembly

Attach 3 of the lengths of twisted cord to the wooden hoop by opening (untwisting) one end of cord and slipping the other end through. Slide the 3 cords into positions at which holding all 3 ends up tog makes the hoop level. At this balance point, knot all 3 cords tog near their tops. Trim off 2 of the cords near the knot, leaving 1 cord above the knot. Sew 1 pom-pom to this cord to cover the knot.

Tip: Once the hoop is balanced and the cords are knotted, I find it helpful to clip the mobile to a high surface so the mobile is hanging while I complete it.

With rem 4 lengths of twisted cord, sew one end to the back of each bunny; play with the attachment location to make the bunny more or less upright when hanging. (Keep in mind whether the baby will be looking up or across the room at it.) Knot other end of each cord to the wooden hoop to hang the 4 bunnies at various lengths and positions. Trim excess cord.

Using clothespins, pin 1 length of rickrack cover to the outside of the hoop, and the second length to the inside of the hoop, matching up the peaks and valleys of the rickrack. Sew the rickrack together along top and bottom edges to cover hoop. This will cover all knots and cords underneath.

Attach rem pom-poms by untwisting cord a little and slipping pom-pom between strands. If necessary, retwist cord to hold the pom-pom or attach with a few stitches.

Wavy Cashmere Blanket

INTERMEDIATE

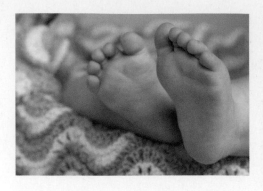

Alternating stripes in a simple feather-and-fan pattern make this blanket look more complicated than it is and creates instant vintage appeal. The cashmere-blend yarn gives a luxurious softness that destines it to be a family heirloom. Choose your own color combinations from the Debbie Bliss range of Baby Cashmerino or use up yarn oddments from your stash—just keep all the yarn the same weight so as not to throw off the gauge.

Finished Measurements

Approximately 35" (89 cm) square (for a larger or smaller blanket, CO a multiple of 18 sts + 2)

Materials

The following 50 g balls DK Debbie Bliss Baby Cashmerino (55% merino, 33% microfiber, 12% cashmere; 137 yds [125 m]):
    5 balls color A: #608 Dusty Lavender
    5 balls color B: #20 Mustard
    5 balls color C: #101 Fresh Cream

US 3 (3.25 mm) 40" (100 cm) circular needle

Yarn needle for finishing

Gauge

27 sts and 32 rows make 4" (10 cm) in pattern

Directions

Tip: You'll need to pay attention to the pattern on the first few rows, but after that you'll see the pattern take shape. Then the stitches will become automatic and quite fun and easy to knit.

Tip: When changing yarn colors, be sure to leave at least a 3" (8 cm) tail of yarn to weave in, but not much more than that so you don't waste precious yarn. Weave the ends in as you go, so you don't have a big job at the end.

Body and Pattern

With color A, CO 236 sts. Check *twice* that you have cast on the right number of stitches before you start knitting.

Row 1 (RS): Knit.

Row 2 (WS): Purl.

Row 3: K1, *(k2tog) 3 times, (yo, k1) 6 times, (k2tog) 3 times; rep from * to last st, k1.

Row 4: Knit.

Rep Rows 1–4, changing color every 4 rows, until blanket measures 35" (89 cm), or desired length.

BO loosely.

Finishing

Weave in ends.

Angora Bolero

INTERMEDIATE / EXPERIENCED

Almost every vintage pattern book has this classic bolero, which was worn over short-sleeved dresses as a stylish little cardigan. The design is perfect for the fluffy softness of angora, which is heaven to knit with, and the merino-angora blend I chose has a great balance of fluff and texture.

Sizes

6–12 months (1–2, 2–3, 3–4 years)

Finished Measurements

Width of back at underarm: 9" (9½", 9¾", 10") (23 [24, 25, 25.5] cm)

Length from back neck: 8" (8½", 9", 9½") (20 [22, 23, 24] cm)

Materials

2 (x, x, x) 50 g balls Sublime Angora Merino (80% wool, 20% angora; 130 yds [119 m]) in #74 Innocent

US 3 (3.25 mm) straight needles

US 6 (4 mm) straight needles

Stitch holder or spare needle

Yarn needle for finishing

Gauge

19 sts and 28 rows make 4" (10 cm) on larger needles in St st

Directions

Right Sleeve

On smaller needles, CO 44 (46, 50, 50) sts. Work 5 rows in garter st.

Next row: *K6 (6, 7, 5), inc1; rep from * to last 2 (4, 2, 2) sts, knit to end—50 (52, 56, 58) sts.

Change to larger needles.

Row 1 (RS): K1, *yo, k2tog; rep from * to last st, k1.

Row 2 (WS): Purl.

Row 3: Rep Row 1.

Row 4: Knit.

Beg with a knit row, work 2 (2, 4, 4) rows in St st.

Right Sleeve Shaping

Inc1 st at each end of next 2 (2, 2, 4) rows. Then CO 3 (4, 4, 4) sts at beg of next 4 rows—66 (72, 76, 82) sts.

Beg with a knit row, work even for 4 rows in St st.

Dec 1 st at beg of every 4th row foll until 63 (69, 73, 79) sts rem.

WS: Purl.

Front Neck

Next row (RS): K30 (33, 35, 38) for front, and turn, leaving rem 33 (36, 38, 41) sts on needle for back.

Next row (WS): BO 6 (6, 6, 8) sts for neck, and purl to end—24 (27, 29, 30) sts.

Next row: K2tog, knit to end.

Next row: P2tog, purl to end.

Rep last 2 rows until 13 (14, 16, 17) sts rem, ending with a RS row. BO.

(continued)

Left Sleeve Shaping

Shape for side edge: BO 3 (4, 4, 4) sts at beg of the next 4 rows, then dec 1 st at each end of next 2 (2, 2, 4) rows—50 (52, 56, 58) sts.

Beg with a knit row, work 3 rows in St st. Then work pattern border as follows:

Row 1 (WS): Knit.

Row 2 (RS): K1, *yo, k2tog; rep from * to last st, k1.

Row 3: Purl.

Row 4: Rep Row 2.

Change to smaller needles.

Next row: *K6 (6, 7, 5), k2tog; rep from * to last 2 (4, 2, 2) sts, knit to end—44 (46, 50, 50) sts.

Work 5 more rows in garter st. BO.

Front Edging

On smaller needles and with RS facing, beg at lower side edge of right front, pick up evenly and k128 (136, 142, 150) sts around side, front, and back edges to lower side edge of left front. Work these sts as follows:

Row 1 (WS): Knit.

Row 2 (RS): K1, *yo, k2tog; rep from * to last st, k1.

Row 3: Purl.

Row 4: Rep Row 2.

Left Front

On larger needles, CO 13 (14, 16, 17) sts.

Row 1 (RS): Inc1, knit to end.

Row 2 (WS): Inc1, purl to end.

Rep Rows 1–2 until you have 24 (27, 29, 30) sts on needle, ending with a RS row.

CO 6 (6, 6, 8) sts at beg of next row, and purl to end—30 (33, 35, 38). Knit 1 row even. Sl sts onto stitch holder or spare needle.

Back

With RS facing, join yarn to the 33 (36, 38, 41) sts for back, and work 30 (34, 36, 38) rows in St st, ending with a knit row.

Left Sleeve

Next row (WS): P across all 33 (36, 38, 41) sts of back and then across all 30 (33, 35, 38) sts of left front—63 (69, 73, 79) sts.

Inc1 st at beg of every 4th row foll until you have 66 (72, 76, 82) sts, then work 4 rows even.

Row 5: Knit.

Work 5 more rows in garter st. BO.

Back Edging

On smaller needles and with RS facing, pick up evenly and k30 (34, 36, 38) sts along back bottom edge; work in pattern given for front edging. BO.

Finishing

Join side and underarm seams. Press seams very lightly with a warm iron and a damp cloth. Weave in ends.

Organic Heirloom Blanket

BEGINNER

This little swaddling blanket knits up quickly. Sumptuously soft organic cotton is ideal for babies with sensitive skin or allergies to wool. The simple eyelet pattern appeals to boys and girls alike, and the blankie is sure to be a favorite for years.

Finished Measurements

Approximately 30" (76 cm) square

Materials

4 100 g skeins Blue Sky Alpacas Dyed Organic Cotton (100% cotton; 150 yds [137 m]) in #604 Aloe

US 8 (5 mm) 24" (60 cm) circular needle

Yarn needle for finishing

Gauge

16 sts and 25 rows make 4" (10 cm) in pattern

Directions

Tip: You'll need to pay attention to the pattern for the first few rows, but after that, the stitches will become automatic and quite fun and easy to knit.

CO 125 sts. Check *twice* that you have cast on the right number of stitches before you start knitting.

Knit 9 rows.

Work pattern:

Row 1 (RS): Knit.

Rows 2, 4, 6, and 8 (WS): K7, p to last 7 sts, k7.

Row 3: K7, *k2, k2tog, yo; rep from * to last 9 sts, knit to end.

Row 5: Rep Row 1.

Row 7: K7, *k2tog, yo, k2; rep from * to last 9 sts, k2tog, yo, knit to end.

Repeat Rows 1–8 until blanket measures 29" (74 cm).

Knit 9 rows.

BO.

Weave in ends.

Modern Baby Bonnet

Who wouldn't adore a sweet little classic baby bonnet modernized by simple detailing and yummy cashmere-merino-silk yarn—a bit of luxury for today's baby.

Sizes

0–3 (3–6, 6–12) months

Finished Measurements

Height: 6" (6½", 7") (15 [16.5, 18] cm)

Materials

1 (1, 1) 50 g ball Sublime Baby Cashmere Merino Silk DK (75% extra-fine merino wool, 20% silk, 5% cashmere; 127 yds [116 m]) in #02 Cuddle

US 6 (4 mm) straight needles

Yarn needle for finishing and attaching button

1 (½" [1.5 cm]) button

Gauge

22 sts and 28 rows make 4" (10 cm) in St st pattern

Directions

Cap

CO 68 (72, 76) sts.

Rows 1–6: *K1, p1; rep from * to end.

Row 7 (RS): *K2, p2; rep from * to end.

Row 8 (WS): *K2, p2; rep from * to end.

Row 9: *P2, k2; rep from * to end.

Row 10: *P2, k2; rep from * to end.

Rep Rows 7–10 until work measures 4" (4¾", 5") (10 [12, 13] cm) from beg, ending with a WS row, and inc 4 (2, 0) sts evenly across last row—72 (74, 76) sts.

Back Shaping

Row 1 (RS): K0 (1, 2), *sl2k, k14, k2tog; rep from * 3 times, k0 (1, 2)—64 (66, 68) sts.

Row 2 and all even rows (WS): Purl.

Row 3: K0 (1, 2), *sl2k, k12, k2tog; rep from * 3 times, k0 (1, 2)—56 (58, 60) sts.

Row 5: K0 (1, 2), *sl2k, k10, k2tog; rep from * 3 times, k0 (1, 2)—48 (50, 52) sts.

(continued)

Row 7: K0 (1, 2), *sl2k, k8, k2tog; rep from * 3 times, k0 (1, 2)—40 (42, 44) sts.

Row 9: K0 (1, 2), *sl2k, k6, k2tog; rep from * 3 times, k0 (1, 2)—32 (34, 36) sts.

Row 11: K0 (1, 2), *sl2k, k4, k2tog; rep from * 3 times, k0 (1, 2)—24 (26, 28) sts.

Row 13: K0 (1, 2), *sl2k, k2, k2tog; rep from * 3 times, k0 (1, 2)—16 (18, 20) sts.

Row 15: *K2tog; rep from * to end—8 (9, 10) sts.

Break yarn, thread through rem sts, pull tight, and fasten off.

Band

CO 9 sts.

Row 1: *K1, p1; rep from * to last st, k1.

Row 2: *P1, k1; rep from * to last st, p1.

Rep Rows 1–2 until band measures 11½" (12", 12½") (29 [30.5, 32] cm]).

Next row (buttonhole): Rib 4, yo, k2tog, rib to end.

Next 3 rows: Cont in rib, and k2tog at beg and end of row—3 sts.

Work 1 row in rib.

K3tog. Fasten off.

Finishing

Stitch back seam of cap together. Attach band around base of cap, leaving buttonhole end 2" (5 cm) of band free at right front. Sew button on cap. Weave in ends.

Vintage Pixie Cap

An easy-to-knit hat creates instant vintage style with its charming peaked hood. Babies love to wear this cap in cashmere-merino blend and can't tug it off because of the handy button strap.

Sizes

3–6 months (6–12 months, 1–2 years, 2–3 years)

Finished Measurements

Height: 6" (6¼", 6½", 7") (15 [16, 16.5, 18] cm)

Materials

1 (1, 1, 1) 50 g ball Debbie Bliss Cashmerino DK (55% merino wool, 33% microfiber, 12% cashmere; 125 yds [114 m]) in #04 Red

US 6 (4 mm) straight needles

Removable marker

1 (⅝" [16 mm]) button

Needle and thread to match yarn

Gauge

22 sts and 30 rows make 4" (10 cm) in St st

Directions

Cap

CO 64 (68, 72, 78) sts.

Rows 1–6: *K1, p1; rep from * to end.

Change to St st, and work even until work measures 5½" (6", 7", 7½") (14 [15, 17.5, 19] cm) from beg.

BO.

Strap

CO 7 sts.

Row 1: K2, *p1, k1; rep from * once, k1.

Row 2: *K1, p1; rep from * twice, k1.

Rep Rows 1–2 until strap measures 9" (9½", 10", 10½") (23 [24, 25.5, 26.5] cm). Place marker in edge of work.

Cont in rib for a further 1" (1½", 2", 2¼") (3 [4, 5, 6] cm), ending with Row 1.

Next row (buttonhole): Rib 3, yo, k2tog, rib to end.

Rib 3 rows.

BO.

Finishing

Fold cap in half with ribbing at front, and join bound-off edges to form back seam.

Join strap to cap (as far as marker) around lower edge of cap, easing in fullness of cap.

Attach button. Weave in ends.

Wee Mittens

BEGINNER / INTERMEDIATE

These classic, simply made vintage mittens are the same for right and left hands, which eliminates hassle while dressing little ones. Say good-bye to itchy wrists, thanks to a scrumptious blended yarn. Add your own embellishments—vintage buttons, embroidery, stripes, whatever you fancy.

Tip: To keep mittens from getting lost, sew one end of a 30" (76 cm) ribbon or twisted cord to each mitten cuff, and pull the mittens through the sleeves of baby's coat—just like Nana used to do!

Sizes

0–12 months (1–3 years)

Materials

1 (1) 50 g ball Debbie Bliss Cashmerino DK (55% merino wool, 33% microfiber, 12% cashmere; 125 yds [114 m]) in #04 Red

US 5 (3.75 mm) straight needles

US 6 (4 mm) straight needles

2 stitch markers

Yarn needle for finishing

Gauge

22 sts and 30 rows make 4" (10 cm) with larger needles in St st

Directions (Make 2)

Cuff

With smaller needles, loosely CO 27 (31) sts.

Row 1 (RS): *K1, p1; rep from * to last st, k1.

Row 2 (WS): *P1, k1; rep from * to last st, p1.

Rep Rows 1–2 until you have 10 (12) rows of rib.

Change to larger needles, and work 2 (2) rows in St st.

Thumb Gusset

Row 1 (RS): K13 (15), place marker, M1, k1, M1, place marker, knit to end—29 (33) sts.

Row 2 (WS): Purl.

Row 3: K to marker, sl marker, M1, k to marker, M1, sl marker, knit to end—31 (35) sts.

Rep Rows 2–3 until you have 11 (13) sts between markers.

Next row: Purl.

Thumb

Row 1: K24 (28), turn.

Row 2: P4 (5), p2tog, p5 (6), turn.

Work 2 (4) rows in St st on these 10 (12) sts.

Next Row: K2tog 5 (6) times—5 (6) sts.

Break yarn, thread tail through rem sts, and pull tight.

Top Shaping

Rejoin yarn to sts on left needle with RS facing, and knit to end—26 (30) sts.

Cont in St st until work measures 4½" (4¾") (11.5 [12] cm) from beg, ending with a purl row.

Row 1 (RS): *K2, k2tog; rep from * to last 2 sts, k2—20 (23) sts.

Row 2 (WS): Purl.

Row 3: Rep Row 1—14 (16) sts.

Row 4: Purl.

Row 5: *K2tog; rep from * to end—7 (8) sts.

Break yarn, leaving an 18" (46 cm) tail. Thread tail onto yarn needle, run needle through rem sts. Slip sts off needle, pull yarn tight, and fasten securely. Leave long yarn end for sewing up.

Finishing

Fold mitten with RS tog and sew seams using a mattress st.

Anya's Cardigan

INTERMEDIATE / EXPERIENCED

This timeless cardigan, with delicate eyelet pattern, raglan sleeves, and stylish front bands, was inspired by a collection of sweaters my friend's grandmother had knitted for her when she was a baby (see page 1). More than thirty years later, her daughters could wear them, looking as beautiful as the day they were made. It is knitted in silky soft merino-cotton blend, for light weight, and is worked simply in one piece to the armhole.

Sizes

0–3 (3–6, 6–12, 12–24) months

Finished Measurements

Chest width (buttoned): 19½" (22", 24", 26") (49.5 [56, 61, 66] cm)

Length from back neck: 9½" (10½", 11½", 13") (24 [26.5, 29, 33] cm)

Sleeve seam: 6" (7", 8", 9") (15 [17.5, 20.5, 23] cm)

Materials

2 (3, 3, 4) 50 g balls Rowan Wool Cotton (50% merino wool, 50% cotton; 127 yds [116 m]) in #900 Antique

US 3 (3.25 mm) straight needles

US 5 (3.75 mm) straight needles

2 safety pins

Stitch holders

Yarn needle for finishing

5 (½" [13 mm]) buttons

Needle and matching thread for sewing on buttons

Gauge

22 sts and 30 rows make 4" (10 cm) on larger needles in St st

Directions

Body (1 Piece to Armhole)

On smaller needles, CO 113 (125, 137, 149) sts.

Row 1: K1, *p1, k1; rep from * to end.

Row 2: P1, *k1, p1; rep from * to end.

Rows 3–4: Rep Rows 1–2.

Row 5 (buttonhole): K1, p1, yo, p2tog, rib to end.

Rows 6–9: Work in rib.

Row 10: Rib 5, sl those sts onto a safety pin for front band, rib to last 5 sts, turn; slip rem 5 sts onto a safety pin.

Change to larger needles, and work pattern on rem 103 (115, 127, 139) sts as follows:

Row 1 (RS): Knit.

Row 2 (WS): P2, *k3, p3; rep from * to last 5 sts, k3, p2.

Row 3: K3, *yo, k2tog, k4; rep from * to last 4 sts, yo, k2tog, k2.

Row 4: Rep Row 2.

(continued)

Row 5: Knit.

Row 6: K2, *p3, k3; rep from * to last 5 sts, p3, k2.

Row 7: K6, *yo, k2tog, k4; rep from * to last st, k1.

Row 8: Rep Row 6.

Rep Rows 1–8 until work measures 5½" (6", 6½", 7½") (14 [15, 16.5, 19] cm) from beg, ending with a WS row.

Right Front

Row 1 (RS): Work 25 (28, 31, 34) sts in pattern, turn, and work on these sts only.

Row 2 (WS): BO 2 sts, work pattern to end—23 (26, 29, 32) sts.

Row 3: Work pattern to last 3 sts, k2tog, k1—22 (25, 28, 31) sts.

Row 4: P2, work pattern to end.

Rep Rows 3–4 until 13 (15, 16, 17) sts rem, ending with a WS row.

Right Front Neck Shaping

Next row (RS): BO 3 (3, 4, 5) sts, work pattern to last 3 sts, k2tog, k1—9 (11, 11, 11) sts.

Next row (WS): P2, work pattern to end.

Next row: Sl1, k1, psso, work pattern to last 3 sts, k2tog, k1—2 sts dec'd.

Rep last 2 rows until 3 sts rem, ending with a WS row.

Next row: K2tog, k1.

P2tog, fasten off.

Back

With RS facing, rejoin yarn to rem 78 (87, 96, 105) sts.

Row 1 (RS): BO 2 sts, work sts in pattern until you have 51 (57, 63, 69) sts on right needle, turn, and work on these sts only.

Row 2 (WS): BO 2 sts, work pattern to end—49 (55, 61, 67) sts.

Row 3: K1, k2tog tbl, work pattern to last 3 sts, k2tog, k1—47 (53, 59, 65) sts.

Row 4: P2, work pattern to last 2 sts, p2.

Rep Rows 3–4 rows until 19 (21, 23, 25) sts rem.

Sl sts onto stitch holder for neckband.

Left Front

With RS facing, rejoin yarn to rem 25 (28, 31, 34) sts.

Row 1 (RS): BO 2 sts, work pattern to end—23 (26, 29, 32) sts.

Row 2 (WS): Work pattern to last 2 sts, p2.

Row 3: K1, k2tog tbl, work pattern to end—1 st dec'd.

Rep Rows 2–3 until 13 (15, 16, 17) sts rem, ending with a RS row.

Left Front Neck Shaping

Next row (WS): BO 3 (3, 4, 5) sts, work pattern to last 2 sts, p2—10 (12, 12, 12) sts.

Next row (RS): K1, k2tog tbl, work pattern to last 2 sts, k2tog—2 sts dec'd.

Next row: Work pattern to last 2 sts, p2.

Rep last 2 rows until 4 sts rem.

Next row (RS): K1, k2tog tbl, k1—3 sts.

Next row: Purl.

Next row: K1, k2tog tbl.

Next row: P2tog, BO.

Sleeve (Make 2)

On smaller needles, CO 25 (31, 31, 31) sts, and work k1, p1 rib for 1½" (4 cm) as for body.

Change to larger needles, and work in pattern, beg with Row 1 (RS), inc 1 st at each end of every 4th (5th, 5th, 5th) row, working inc sts into pattern, until you have 39 (43, 47, 51) sts.

Work even until sleeve measures 6" (7", 8", 9") (15 [17.5, 20.5, 23] cm) from beg, ending with a WS row.

Shape Sleeve Top

CO 2 sts at beg of next 2 rows—35 (39, 43, 47) sts.

Row 1 (RS): K1, k2tog tbl, work pattern to last 3 sts, k2tog, k1—33 (37, 42, 47) sts.

Row 2 (WS): P2, work pattern to last 2 sts, p2.

Rep Rows 1–2 until 5 sts rem. Sl sts onto a stitch holder.

Front Bands

On smaller needles, with WS of work facing, rejoin yarn to 5 sts on safety pin at right front.

Work in rib, making 3 more buttonholes, 1¾" (2", 2¼", 2½") (4.5 [5, 5.5, 6.5] cm) from 1st buttonhole already made and from one another.

Work even for 1½" (2", 2¼", 2½") (4 [4.5, 5, 6] cm), and sl sts onto a stitch holder for neckband.

With RS of work facing, rejoin yarn to 5 sts on safety pin at left front, and work band the same length as right front band but without buttonholes.

Neck Band

Join raglan seams.

With RS of work facing, rib across sts on right front band, pick up evenly and k11 (12, 13, 14) sts from right front neck, k across sts on sleeve tops and back neck

stitch holders, pick up evenly and k11 (12, 13, 14) sts down left front neck, and rib across sts on left front band—61 (65, 69, 73) sts.

Work 4 more rows in rib, making buttonhole on Row 2.

BO in rib.

Finishing

Press pieces lightly with a warm iron and damp cloth. Join sleeve seams. Sew front bands into position, and sew on buttons. Weave in ends.

Cabled Booties

Super cozy little boots with easy mock cables can be personalized with custom fabric-covered buttons for vintage appeal. The pure wool keeps little toes toasty warm inside and out.

Sizes

0–3 (3–6, 6–12) months

Materials

1 (1, 1) 50 g ball Jo Sharp DK Wool (100% wool; 107 yds [98 m]) in #355 Paris

US 3 (3.25 mm) straight needles

US 6 (4 mm) straight needles

Yarn needle for finishing

2 (⅜" [18 mm]) cloth-covered buttons (see page 12)

Needle and matching thread for sewing on buttons

Gauge

22 sts and 30 rows make 4" (10 cm) on larger needles in St st

Tip: You will end up with two small "holes" in the top on both sides of the bootie. The holes will be covered with the strap when it is sewn on.

Directions

Booties (Make 2)

Begin at center of sole.

On larger needles, CO 31 (35, 39) sts.

Rows 1, 3, 5, 7: Knit.

Row 2: K1, inc1, k12 (14, 16), inc1, k1, inc1, k12 (14, 16), inc1, k1—35 (39, 43) sts.

Row 4: K1, inc1, k14 (16, 18), inc1, k1, inc1, k14 (16, 18), inc1, k1—39 (43, 47) sts.

Row 6: K1, inc1, k16 (18, 20), inc1, k1, inc1, k16 (18, 20), inc1, k1—43 (47, 51) sts.

Row 8: K1, inc1, k18 (20, 22), inc1, k1, inc1, k18 (20, 22), inc1, k1—47 (51, 55) sts

Knit even for 5 (7, 9) rows.

Instep Shaping

Row 1 (RS): K28 (29, 32), k2tog tbl, turn.

Row 2: Sl1, p7 (8, 9), p2tog, turn.

Row 3: Sl1, k7 (8, 9), k2tog tbl, turn.

Row 4: Sl1, p7 (8, 9), p2tog, turn.

Rep Rows 3–4 until 29 (33, 37) sts rem.

Next row: Sl1, k7 (8, 9), k2tog tbl, knit to end—28 (32, 36) sts.

Next row: Purl to end.

Cable Leg Pattern

Tip: To work C2B or C2F, knit into the back (or front) of the second stitch on the left needle, then knit the first stitch, and slip both stitches off the needle together.

Row 1 (RS): K1, *C2B, p2; rep from * to last 3 sts, C2B, k1.

Row 2 (WS): P1, *p2, k2; rep from * to last 3 sts, p3.

Row 3: K1, *C2F, p2; rep from * to last 3 sts, C2F, k1.

Row 4: P1, *p2, k2; rep from * to last 3 sts, p3.

Rep Rows 1–4 until leg measures 2" (2¾", 2¾") (5 [7, 7] cm), ending with a RS row.

BO loosely.

Strap

On smaller needles, CO 4 sts, and work 18 (20, 22) rows garter st. BO.

Finishing

Join seams. Sew fabric-covered button to strap and strap to top of instep on each bootie, as shown in photo. For babies with thin ankles, sew strap across bootie tightly. Weave in ends.

Baby Clothes Hanger Covers

BEGINNER

Use bits of leftover yarn to knit up little hanger covers in a flash and have fun embellishing them with your favorite ribbon or buttons. Not only do they add charm to a baby's room but they also keep tiny clothes from slipping off the hanger. They make a lovely last-minute gift idea for a baby shower.

Materials

Balls of leftover light worsted or DK-weight yarn

US 9 (5.5 mm) straight needles

Plain 12" (30 cm) wooden hangers (available in craft stores)

Bits of ribbon or buttons for decoration

Yarn needle for finishing

Needle and thread to match yarn or decorations

Gauge

Not important for this pattern

Directions

Tip: You knit the hanger cover as a long, narrow rectangle just a bit shorter than your hanger length, because the cover can be stretched to fit snugly when you stitch it together at the bottom. Poke the metal hook through the middle of the rectangle before stitching.

With 2 strands of yarn together, CO 9 sts, and work in garter st until work measures 9" (23 cm). BO, leaving a 12" (30 cm) tail for sewing together.

Poke hanger's metal hook through middle of cover's length and width, so that knitting lies along top of hanger. Using yarn tail, sew cover's side and bottom edges together, using mattress stitch or whipstitch. Tuck in loose ends as you go. Embellish with buttons or ribbon as desired.

Apron Dress

A classic little girl's pinafore with modern styling can be worn over tops and with pants to give baby an extra layer of warmth when needed. As baby grows, knit the next size up and adjust the buttons, to lengthen the pinafore. At first it is a dress; gradually, it becomes a tunic.

Sizes

3–6 months (6–12 months, 1–2 years, 2–3 years)

Finished Measurements

Chest width: 21" (22½", 24½", 26") (53.5 [57, 62, 66] cm)

Length from back neck: 10" (11¾", 13¼", 15½") (25.5 [30, 33.5, 39.5] cm)

Materials

4 (5, 5, 6) balls Sublime Cashmere Merino Silk DK (75% extra-fine merino, 20% silk, 5% cashmere; 127 yds [116 m]) in #56 Mole

US 6 (4 mm) straight needles

US 6 (4 mm) 16" circular needles

2 safety pins

Stitch holders

Yarn needle for finishing

2 (¾" [2 cm]) buttons

Needle and thread to match yarn

Gauge

22 sts and 28 rows make 4" (10 cm) in St st

Directions

Back

With straight needles, CO 68 (70, 74, 78) sts.

Rows 1–5: Knit.

Row 6 (WS): Purl.

Row 7 (dec row) (RS): K1, sl1, k1, psso, knit to last 3 sts, k2tog, k1—66 (68, 72, 76) sts.

Cont in St st, rep Row 7 every foll 6th (8th, 10th, 12th) row, until 58 (62, 68, 72) sts rem. Work even until work measures 6½" (8", 9", 11") (16.5 [20, 23, 28] cm) from beg, ending with a WS row.

Armhole Shaping

BO 4 sts at beg of next 2 rows—50 (54, 60, 64) sts.

Dec 1 st at each end of next row and every 2nd row until 38 (42, 46, 50) sts rem.**

Work 13 (15, 17, 19) rows even.

Back Neck Shaping

Next row (RS): K12 (13, 14, 15), turn. Cont on these sts for shoulder flap.

Next 3 rows: Dec 1 st at neck edge, ending with 9 (10, 11, 12) sts.

Next 6 rows: Work even.

Next 2 rows: Dec 1 st at each end, ending with 5 (6, 7, 8) sts.

Slip those sts onto a safety pin.

Sl next 14 (16, 18, 20) sts onto a stitch holder.

With RS facing, rejoin yarn to rem 12 (13, 14, 15) sts. Work to match 1st shoulder flap, reversing shaping.

(continued)

Pocket Lining (Make 2)

CO 15 (17, 17, 19) sts.

Beg with a knit row, work 12 (18, 18, 20) rows in St st. Sl sts onto a stitch holder.

Next row: *K1, p1; rep from * to end.

Rep last row 3 times more. Sl sts onto a stitch holder.

Front

Work same as back to **, except place pockets as follows:

Row 19 (25, 25, 27): K4 (5, 6, 7), sl next 15 (17, 17, 19) sts onto a stitch holder for pocket bottom edge; in their place, pick up and k15 (17, 17, 19) sts of one pocket lining from stitch holder. Knit to last 19 (22, 23, 26) sts. Sl next 15 (17, 17, 19) sts onto a holder for second pocket. Pick up and k15 (17, 17, 19) sts of other pocket lining from stitch holder, knit to end.

Front Neck Shaping

Next Row: K14 (16, 17, 19), turn.

Cont on these sts for side of neck.

Dec 1 st at neck edge on every RS row until 10 (11, 14, 16) sts rem, then on every 4th row until 9 (10, 11, 12) sts rem. Purl all WS rows.

Next 2 rows (RS and WS): Dec 1 st at each end, ending with 5 (6, 7, 8) sts.

Slip rem sts onto a safety pin.

Sl next 10 (10, 12, 12) sts onto a stitch holder.

With RS facing, rejoin yarn to rem 14 (16, 17, 19) sts. Complete to match 1st front neck side, reversing shaping.

Change to circular needles.

Front Neck and Armhole Edging

With RS facing, starting at right side, pick up evenly and k24 (28, 34, 38) sts around armhole shaping, k5 (6, 7, 8) sts from safety pin, pick up evenly and k12 (16, 22, 30) sts along front neck shaping, k10 (10, 12, 12) sts from front neck stitch holder as you dec 2 sts evenly spaced, pick up evenly and k12 (16, 22, 30) sts along front neck shaping, k5 (6, 7, 8) sts from safety pin, then pick up evenly and k24 (28, 34, 38) sts around armhole shaping—90 (108, 136, 162) sts.

Knit 1 row. BO knitwise.

Back Neck and Armhole Edging

With RS facing, from right edge, pick up evenly and k24 (28, 34, 38) sts around armhole, k5 (6, 7, 8) sts from safety pin, pick up evenly and k12 sts along back neck shaping, k14 (16, 18, 20) sts from back neck stitch holder, dec 2 sts evenly spaced, pick up evenly and k12 sts along back neck shaping, k across 5 (6, 7, 8) sts from safety pin, pick up evenly and k24 (28, 34, 38) sts around armhole—94 (106, 122, 134) sts.

Next row (buttonholes): K26 (30, 37, 42), yo, k2tog, k38 (42, 44, 46), k2tog, yo, k26 (30, 37, 42).

BO knitwise.

Pocket Edging (Make 2)

Using straight needles, Sl 15 (17, 17, 19) sts from holder of one pocket edge onto needle.

With RS facing, rejoin yarn. Work 6 rows in k1, p1 rib.

BO. Sew in place on inside.

Finishing

Join side seams. Sew on buttons. Weave in ends.

Ballet Blossom Cardigan

INTERMEDIATE / EXPERIENCED

Wonderfully warm baby alpaca wraps baby in softness. Simple raglan sleeves and a knit flower add delicate detailing to this feminine little cardigan for tiny ballerinas.

The blossom pattern on page 66, © Nicky Epstein, is reprinted from *Nicky Epstien's Knitted Flowers* with permission from the author and Sixth&Spring Books.

Sizes

6–12 (12–24) months

Finished Measurements

Chest width (closed): 19" (21") (48 [53.5] cm)

Length from back neck: 9½" (10½") (24 [26.5] cm)

Sleeve seam: 6" (6¾") (15 [16.5] cm)

Materials

3 (4) 50 g balls RYC Baby Alpaca DK (100% baby alpaca; 109 yds [100 m]) in #200 Blossom

US 3 (3.25 mm) straight needles

US 5 (3.75 mm) straight needles

US 6 (4 mm) straight needles

Removable markers

Yarn needle for finishing and attaching button and blossom

1 button for flower center

Gauge

24 sts and 32 rows make 4" (10 cm) on US 6 (4 mm) needles in St st

Directions

Work front edge decs as follows:

On left front: RS rows, k to last 3 sts, k2tog, k1; WS rows, p1, p2tog, purl to end.

On right front: RS rows, k1, sl1, k1, psso, knit to end; WS rows, p to last 3 sts, p2tog tbl, p1.

Left Front

On US 3 (3.25 mm) needles, CO 57 (63) sts.

Row 1: K1, *p1, k1; rep from * to end.

Row 2: P1, *k1, p1; rep from * to end.

Rep Rows 1–2 for 1" (2.5 cm), ending with Row 2.**

Change to US 5 (3.75 mm) needles.

Work 0 (2) rows in St st, beg with a knit row. Place a marker at beg of last row, to mark front edge.

Cont in St st, dec 1 st at marked edge on next row (RS) and every alt row foll until 53 (59) sts rem.

Dec 1 st at marked edge on every row until 28 (32) sts rem, ending with a purl row.

Work should measure 5" (5½") (12.5 [14] cm) from beg.

Left Raglan Shaping

Next row (RS): BO 3 sts, k to last 3 sts, k2tog, k1—24 (27) sts.

Next row (WS): Purl.

Next row: K to last 3 sts, k2tog, k1.

Next row: Purl.

Next row: K1, sl1, k1, psso, k to last 3 sts, k2tog, k1.

**Cont to dec 1 st at armhole edge every 4th row foll, and, *at the same time*, dec 1 st at marked edge every 2nd row foll until 18 (21) sts rem, ending with a purl row.

Then dec 1 st at armhole edge every other row foll, and, *at the same time*, dec 1 st at marked edge every 4th row foll until 6 sts rem.

Then work even at marked edge, and dec 1 st only at armhole edge every other row until 2 sts rem, ending with a purl row. K2tog, fasten off.**

Right Front

Work same as left front to raglan shaping, except place marker at *end* of 1st row of St st to mark front edge.

Right Raglan Shaping

Next row (RS): K1, sl1, k1, psso, knit to end.

Next row (WS): BO 3 sts, purl to end— 24 (27) sts.

(continued)

Next row: K1, sl1, k1, psso, knit to end.

Next row: Purl.

Next row: K1, sl1, k1, psso, k to last 3 sts, k2tog, k1.

Work from ** to ** of left raglan shaping.

Back

On US 3 (3.25 mm) needles, CO 57 (63) sts. Work k1, p1 rib as for left front for 1" (2.5 cm).

Change to US 5 (3.75 mm) needles. Work in St st, beg with a knit row, until back measures same to armhole as left front, ending with a purl row.

Back Raglan Shaping

BO 3 sts at beg of next 2 rows—51 (57) sts.

Work 2 rows even.

Next row (RS): K1, sl1, k1, psso, k to last 3 sts, k2tog, k1.

Work 3 rows even.

Dec 1 st at each end on next row and every 4th row foll until 45 (51) sts rem, then on every other row foll until 23 (25) sts rem, ending with a purl row. BO.

Sleeve (Make 2)

On US 3 (3.25 mm) needles, CO 33 (35) sts.

Work in k1, p1 rib as for left front for 1" (2.5 cm).

Change to US 5 (3.75 mm) needles.

Work in St st, beg with a knit row, inc 1 st at each end on the 5th row and every 4th row foll, until you have 39 (41) sts, then inc 1 st at each end every 6th row foll, until you have 45 (49) sts.

Work even until sleeve measures 6" (6¾") (15 [17] cm) from beg, ending with a purl row.

Sleeve Top Shaping

BO 3 sts at beg of next 2 rows—39 (43) sts.

Next row (RS): K1, sl1, k1, psso, k to last 3 sts, k2tog, k1.

Next row (WS): P1, p2tog, p to last 3 sts, p2tog tbl, p1—35 (39) sts.

Next row: K1, sl1, k1, psso, k to last 3 sts, k2tog, k1—33 (37) sts.

Next row: Purl.

Rep last 2 rows until 5 sts rem, ending with a purl row.

Next row: K1, sl2, k1, psso, k1—3 sts.

Next row: Purl.

BO.

Press pieces lightly with a warm iron and a damp cloth. Sew raglan seams. Sew left side and sleeve seam.

Blossom

Wind a few yards (meters) of yarn into a separate mini-ball 2 times. On US 6 (4 mm) needles, CO 3 sts with 1 ball of yarn (main ball or mini-ball). With separate ball of yarn, CO 3 sts on same needle—6 sts total.

Row 1 (RS): *K1, CO 1, k1, CO 1, k1; rep from * on 2nd set of sts with 2nd ball of yarn—5 sts each set.

Row 2 (WS): Purl.

Row 3: *K1, CO 1, k3, CO1, k1; rep from * on 2nd set of sts—7 sts each set.

Row 4: Join the 2 sets of sts as foll: P6, p2tog, p6—13 sts. Cut off yarn ball not used for this row, and fasten end. Cont with rem attached yarn ball.

Row 5: *K1, CO 1, k11, CO 1, k1—15 sts.

Rows 6, 8, 10, 12, and 14: Purl.

Row 7: K6, sl2, k1, psso, k6—13 sts.

Row 9: K5, sl2, k1, psso, k5—11 sts.

Row 11: Sl2k, k2, sl2, k1, psso, k2, k2tog—7 sts.

Row 13: Sl2k, sl2, k1, psso, k2tog—3 sts.

Leave sts for this petal on needle. Cont on same needles to make 3 more petals—12 sts total on needle.

Purl 1 row connecting 4 petals. Do not fasten off last yarn tail.

With yarn needle, pass tail through rem sts on needle, pull tight, and secure. Fasten off other yarn ends. Sew button to center.

Front Band

On US 3 (3.25 mm) needles, CO 7 sts.

Work in rib same as left front until band measures 8" (20.5 cm). Place a marker in last row. Cont in rib until band is long enough from marker when slightly stretched to fit up right front, across back neck, and down left front to bottom edge.

Place a second marker in last row.

Cont in rib until band is 16" (40.5 cm) more from second marker.

BO in rib. Sew band in place, leaving 8" (20 cm) loose at right side and 16" (40 cm) loose at left side.

Finishing

Join right side seam by backstitching, leaving a ½" (1 cm) opening above rib. Sew right sleeve seam. Attach blossom to right front of sweater with button at center. Weave in ends. Thread left front tie (16" [40.5 cm] left loose at left side of front band) through opening at right side seam, take round back of garment and tie at left side to 8" (20 cm) left loose at right side.

Charming Raglan Pullover

INTERMEDIATE / EXPERIENCED

Inspired by a vintage pattern, this classic baby pullover has lovely eyelet raglan sleeves and a delicate pattern edging. Delightful for baby boys as well as girls, it has tiny buttons at the back opening, so that baby (and parents) need not struggle to pull it on or off. Naturally soft and sturdy pure wool retains its shape through years of wear.

Sizes

3–6 months (6–12 months, 1–2 years, 2–3 years)

Finished Measurements

Chest width: 16" (19", 21½", 24") (40.5 [48.5, 54.5, 61] cm)

Length from back neck: 10" (11", 12", 13") (25.5 [28, 30.5, 33] cm)

Sleeve seam: 5" (5½", 6½", 7½") (12.5 [14, 16.5, 19] cm)

Materials

3 (4, 4, 5) balls Jo Sharp DK Wool (100% wool; 107 yds [98 m]) in #906 Orchard

US 3 (3.25 mm) straight needles

US 5 (3.75 mm) straight needles

Stitch holders

Yarn needle for finishing

3 (½" [13 mm]) buttons

Needle and thread to match yarn

Gauge

24 sts and 32 rows make 4" (10 cm) on larger needles in St st

Directions

Back

On smaller needles, CO 49 (57, 65, 73) sts.

Row 1: K1, *p1, k1; rep from * to end.

Row 2: P1, *k1, p1; rep from * to end.

Rep Rows 1–2 until rib measures 1" (2.5 cm), ending with Row 2.

Change to larger needles, and work pattern as follows:

Row 1 (RS): K1, *yo, k2, sl2, k1, psso, k2, yo, k1; rep from * to end.

Rows 2 (WS): Purl.

Row 3: K2, *yo, k1, sl2, k1, psso, k1, yo, k3; rep from * to last 7 sts, yo, k1, sl2, k1, psso, k1, yo, k2.

Row 4: Purl.

Row 5: K3, *yo, sl2, k1, psso, yo, k5; rep from * to last 6 sts, yo, sl2, k1, psso, yo, k3.

Row 6: Purl, inc 2 (0, 0, 0) sts evenly and dec 0 (0, 0, 2) sts evenly—51 (57, 65, 71) sts.

Work in St st, beg with a knit row, until work measures 5" (5½", 6", 6½") (12.5 [14, 15, 16.5] cm) from beg, ending with a purl row.

Raglan Shaping

BO 2 (2, 3, 3) sts at beg of next 2 rows—47 (53, 59, 65) sts.

Next row (RS): K1, k2tog, yo, sl1, k1, psso, k to last 5 sts, k2tog, yo, sl1, k1, psso, k1—2 sts dec'd.

(continued)

Next row (WS): Purl.**

Rep these 2 rows until 43 (45, 47, 49) sts rem.

Back Opening

Next row (RS): K1, k2tog, yo, sl1, k1, psso, k20 (21, 22, 23) sts; turn, and work on these 23 (24, 25, 26) sts only.

Row 1 (WS): K5, purl to end.

Row 2 (RS): K1, k2tog, yo, sl1, k1, psso, knit to end—1 st dec'd.

Rep Rows 1–2 until 11 (12, 13, 14) sts rem, ending with a WS row. *At the same time*, work buttonholes on Rows 9 and 19 (WS) as follows: K2, yo, k2tog, k1, purl to end.

Change to smaller needles, and knit 1 RS row.

Next 2 rows: Work in k1, p1 rib, keeping 5 sts in garter stitch at back opening.

Next row (WS) (buttonhole): K2, yo, k2tog, k1, rib to end.

Next 2 rows: Work in rib with garter st edging.

BO in patterns.

With RS facing, rejoin yarn to rem 19 (20, 21, 22) sts.

Next row: CO 5 sts, k to last 5 sts, k2tog, yo, sl1, k1, psso, k1—23 (24, 25, 26) sts.

Next row (WS): P to last 5 sts, k5.

Next row (RS): K to last 5 sts, k2tog, yo, sl1, k1, psso, k1—1 st dec'd.

Rep last 2 rows until 11 (12, 13, 14) sts rem, ending with a WS row.

Change to smaller needles, and knit 1 RS row.

Next 5 rows: Work in k1, p1 rib, keeping 5 sts in garter st at back opening.

BO in patterns.

Front

Work same as back of sweater to **.

Rep last 2 rows until 33 (35, 39, 41) sts rem.

Neck Shaping

Next row (RS): K1, k2tog, yo, sl1, k1, psso, k9 (9, 11, 11) sts; turn, and work on these 13 (13, 15, 15) sts only.

Next row (WS): Purl.

Next row (RS): K1, k2tog, yo, sl1, k1, psso, k to last 3 sts, k2tog, k1—2 sts dec'd.

Rep last 2 rows until 5 sts rem.

Purl 1 WS row.

Next row: K1, k2tog, yo, sl1, k1, psso, knit to end—4 sts.

Purl 1 row.

Next row: K1, sl1, k1, psso, k1—3 sts.

Purl 1 row.

Next row: K1, sl1, k1, psso—2 sts.

P2tog, and fasten off.

With RS facing, sl center 5 (7, 7, 9) sts onto a stitch holder; rejoin yarn to rem 14 (14, 16, 16) sts, k to last 5 sts, k2tog, yo, sl1, k1, psso, k1—13 (13, 15, 15) sts.

Next row (RS): K1, sl1, k1, psso, k to last 5 sts, k2tog, yo, sl1, k1, psso, k1—2 sts dec'd.

Rep last 2 rows until 5 sts rem.

Purl 1 WS row.

Next row: K2tog, yo, sl1, k1, psso, k1—4 sts.

Purl 1 row.

Next row: K1, k2tog, k1—3 sts.

Purl 1 row.

Next row: K2tog, k1—2 sts.

P2tog, and fasten off.

Sleeve (Make 2)

On smaller needles, CO 31 (33, 37, 39) sts. Work k1, p1 rib same as for back for 1" (2.5 cm).

Next row: Work in rib, inc 2 (0, 4, 2) sts evenly spaced—33 (33, 41, 41) sts.

Change to larger needles, and work Rows 1–5 of pattern as given for back.

Change to St st, beg with a purl row. Inc 1 st at each end of next row (RS) and every 6th (4th, 6th, 4th) row foll until you have 39 (43, 49, 55) sts.

Work even until sleeve measures 5" (5½", 6½", 7½") (12.5 [14, 16.5, 19] cm) from beg, ending with a purl row.

Sleeve Top Shaping

BO 2 (2, 3, 3) sts at beg of next 2 rows—35 (39, 43, 49) sts.

❀ *Sizes 3–6 months, 6–12 months, 1–2 years only:*

Next row (RS): K1, k2tog, yo, sl1, k1, psso, k to last 5 sts, k2tog, yo, sl1, k1, psso, k1—33 (37, 41) sts.

Next row (WS): Purl.

Next row: Knit.

Next row: Purl.

❀ *All sizes:*

Next row (RS): K1, k2tog, yo, sl1, k1, psso, k to last 5 sts, k2tog, yo, sl1, k1, psso, k1—2 sts dec'd.

Next row (WS): Purl.

Rep these 2 rows until 9 sts rem.

Next row (RS): K1, k2tog, yo, sl1, k2tog, psso, yo, sl1, k1, psso, k1—7 sts.

Purl 1 row.

Sl rem sts onto a stitch holder.

Front Neckband

Join front raglan seams.

On smaller needles, with RS facing, k across 7 sts from front left sleeve holder, pick up evenly and k10 (11, 12, 13) sts down left front neck, k across 5 (7, 7, 9) sts from holder at center front, pick up evenly and k10 (11, 12, 13) sts up right front neck, and k across 7 sts from right sleeve holder—39 (43, 45, 49) sts.

Next 5 rows: Work in k1, p1 rib.

BO in rib.

Finishing

Press with a warm iron and a damp cloth. Join back raglan seams. Join side and sleeve seams. Weave in loose ends, and sew on back buttons.

Double-Breasted Car Coat

INTERMEDIATE / EXPERIENCED

This little toddler's coat is gorgeous on boys and girls alike. The soft cashmere-blend yarn is warm and easy to care for.

Sizes

1–2 (2–3) years

Finished Measurements

Chest width (buttoned): 25" (26½") (63.5 [67.5] cm)

Length from back neck: 15" (16½") (38 [42] cm)

Sleeve seam: 6½" (7") (16.5 [18] cm)

Materials

5 (7) 50 g balls RYC Cashsoft DK (57% wool, 33% microfiber, 10% cashmere; 142 yds [130 m]) in #525 Kingfisher

US 6 (4 mm) straight needles

Removable markers

6 (1" [2.5 cm]) buttons

Needle and thread to match yarn

Gauge

22 sts and 30 rows make 4" (10 cm) in St st

Directions

Back

CO 77 (81) sts.

Rows 1–10: *K1, p1; rep from * to last st, k1.

Work in St st, beg with a knit row, until work measures 3" (7.5 cm) from beg. End with a purl row.

Dec 1 st at each end of next row and every 8th row foll until 69 (73) sts rem. Work even until work measures 9" (10") (23 [25.5] cm), ending with a purl row.

Raglan Shaping

BO 2 sts at beg of next 2 rows—65 (69) sts.

Next row (RS): K1, p1, sl1, k1, psso, k to last 4 sts, k2tog, p1, k1.

Next row (WS): K1, purl to last st, k1.

Rep last 2 rows until 19 sts rem.

Work even for 3 rows. BO.

Left Front

CO 47 (51) sts.

Rows 1–9: *K1, p1; rep from * to last st, k1.

Row 10: Cont in seed st, inc1 (0) st at end of row—48 (51) sts.

Row 11 (RS): Knit to last 7 sts, cont seed st for 7 sts.

Row 12 (WS): Seed st 7, purl to end.

Rep Rows 11–12 until work measures 3" (7.5 cm) from beg, ending with a WS row.

Dec 1 st at beg of next row and every 8th row foll until 44 (47) sts rem.

Work even until work measures 9" (10") (23 [25.5] cm), ending with a WS row.

Left Front Raglan Shaping

BO 2 sts at beg of next row—42 (45) sts.

Next row (WS): Work in pattern to last st, k1.

Next row (RS): K1, p1, sl1, k1, psso, work in pattern to end—1 st dec'd.

Rep last 2 rows until 23 (24) sts rem, ending with a RS row.

(continued)

Left Front Neck Shaping

At neck edge, BO 10 (11) sts in Row 1, 3 sts in Row 3, 2 sts in Row 5, and 1 st in Row 7, and at same time cont raglan shaping until 2 sts rem. BO.

Place markers evenly for 3 sets of buttons, the lowest 7½" (8½") (19 [21.5] cm) from CO edge and the topmost ½" (1 cm) below neck edge.

Right Front

To make buttonholes: On RS rows corresponding to markers on left front, work 2 sts, yo twice, k2tog, work 10 sts, yo twice, k2tog, knit to end. When working next row, work double yo as 1 st.

CO 47 (51) sts.

Rows 1–9: *K1, p1; rep from * to last st, k1.

Row 10: Cont in seed st, inc1 (0) st at beg of row—48 (51) sts.

Row 11 (RS): Seed st 7, knit to end.

Row 12 (WS): P to last 7 sts, seed st 7.

Rep rows 11–12 until work measures 3" (7.5 cm) from beg, ending with a WS row.

Dec 1 st at end of next row and every 8th row foll until 44 (47) sts rem.

Work even until work measures 9" (10") (23 [25.5] cm), ending with a RS row.

Right Front Raglan Shaping

BO 2 sts at beg of next row—42 (45) sts.

Next row (RS): Work in pattern to last 4 sts, k2tog, p1, k1—1 st dec'd.

Next row (WS): K1, work in pattern to end.

Rep last 2 rows until 23 (24) sts rem, ending with a WS row.

Right Front Neck Shaping

At neck edge BO 10 (11) sts in Row 1, 3 sts in Row 3, 2 sts in Row 5, and 1 st in Row 7, and at same time cont raglan shaping until 2 sts rem. BO.

Sleeve (Make 2)

CO 41 sts.

Rows 1–10: *K1, p1; rep from * to last st, k1.

Change to St st, beg with a knit row. Inc 1 st at each end of 1st row and every 6th row foll until you have 49 sts; then inc on every 4th row foll until you have 57 (61) sts.

Work even until work measures 6½" (7") (16.5 [18] cm), ending with a purl row.

Sleeve Raglan Shaping

BO 2 sts at beg of next 2 rows—53 (57) sts.

Next row (RS): K1, p1, sl1, k1, psso, k to last 4 sts, k2tog, p1, k1.

Next row (WS): K1, p to last st, k1.

Rep last 2 rows until 7 sts rem.

Work even for 3 rows. BO.

Collar

CO 77 sts.

Rows 1–6: *K1, p1; rep from * to last st, k1.

Row 7 (RS): Work 4 sts in seed st pattern, k to last 4 sts, seed st 4.

Row 8 (WS): Seed st 4, p to last 4 sts, seed st 4.

Rep Rows 7–8 until work measures 2¼" (2½") (5.5 [6] cm), ending with a WS row.

Next row (RS): Seed st 4, k1, *k2tog, k2; rep from * to last 4 sts, seed st 4—60 sts.

Work even for 4 rows.

BO.

Pocket (Make 2)

CO 23 sts.

Rows 1–4: *K1, p1; rep from * to last st, k1.

Row 5 (RS): Seed st 4, k to last 4 sts, seed st 4.

Row 6 (WS): Seed st 4, p to last 4 sts, seed st 4.

Rep Rows 5–6 until work measures 2" (2¼") (5 [5.5] cm), ending with a WS row.

Next row: *K1, p1; rep from * to last st, k1.

Rep last row 4 times more.

BO.

Finishing

Press lightly with a warm iron and a damp cloth. Join side and sleeve seams. Sew on collar 10 sts from front edges. Sew pockets with bottom of pocket 4" (10 cm) from hem and 3" (8 cm) from front edge. Sew on buttons. Weave in ends.

Petite Beret

A simple one-size-fits-all beret can be worn for many seasons, keeping a little head warm and ever so stylish. You may want to knit a couple in different color schemes. I recommend a cashmere blend or fine merino, so the hat is virtually itch free around the child's face. This pattern is good for a beginner who is ready to knit simple decreases and increases.

Size

1–3 years

Finished Measurements

Brim circumference (unstretched): 14" (35.5 cm)

Materials

1 50 g ball RYC Cashsoft DK (57% wool, 33% microfiber, 10% cashmere; 142 yds [130 m]) in #525 Kingfisher

1 50 g ball Debbie Bliss Baby Cashmerino (55% merino wool, 33% microfiber, 12% cashmere; 137 yds [125 m]) in #202 Baby Blue for I-cord

US 3 (3.25 mm) straight needles

US 5 (3.75 mm) straight needles

2 US 5 (3.75 mm) double-pointed needles for I-cord

Yarn needle for finishing

Gauge

24 sts and 32 rows make 4" (10 cm) on larger needles in St st

Directions

Cap

On smaller needles, CO 84 sts loosely.

Rows 1–8: *K1, p1; rep from * to end.

Change to larger needles.

Next row (RS): *(K1, M1) 13 times, (k2, M1) 7 times, k1; rep from * twice more—144 sts.

Next row (WS): Purl.

Next row (eyelets): K4, *yo, k2tog, k2; rep from * to end.

Work even in St st for 15 rows, ending with a purl row.

Crown Shaping

Row 1 (RS): *K16, k2tog; rep from * to end—136 sts.

Row 2 and all even rows (WS): Purl.

Row 3: *K15, k2tog; rep from * to end—128 sts.

Row 5: K14, k2tog; rep from * to end—120 sts.

Row 7: *K13, k2tog; rep from * to end—112 sts.

Cont to dec on every knit row, working 1 fewer st between decs each time, until 24 sts rem.

Next row (WS): Purl.

Next row: *K2tog; rep from * to end—12 sts.

Thread yarn through rem sts, pull tight, and fasten off securely.

I-Cord

On double-pointed needles, CO 3 sts.

Knit across, but don't turn at end of row.

Slide sts to other end of needle, and knit across again.

Cont in this manner, until work is several inches (cm) long; pull down on the knitting, and the gap at the back will close.

Cont until cord is 28" (71 cm) long.

Thread yarn through last sts, pull tight, and fasten off.

Finishing

Using backstitch, join beret seam. Weave in ends. Weave I-cord through eyelets, and tie into a bow at open end.

Tip: For a dressier look, weave a lovely silk or velvet ribbon through the eyelets.

Lavender Sachet

Our grandmothers used scented sachets in their drawers, not only to keep their laundry fresh but also to help ward off moths and other insects. Filled with fragrant herbs, these adorable sachets can also freshen clothes hangers and storage boxes. They are quick to knit and make lovely gifts attached to covered baby clothes hangers (see page 58).

Finished Measurements

Approximately 4" (10 cm) square

Materials

1 65 g skein Blue Sky Alpacas Skinny Organic Cotton (100% cotton; 150 yds [137 m]) in #30 Birch, plus a CC scrap for yarn embroidery

US 3 (3.25 mm) straight needles

Yarn needle for finishing

½ cup (120 ml) dried lavender or any combination of the following herbs: pennyroyal, thyme, mint, chamomile, rosemary, lemon, wormwood

8" (20 cm) of ½" (13 mm)-wide ribbon

Needle and thread to match ribbon

Gauge

24 sts and 47 rows make 4" (10 cm) in garter st

Directions

CO 25 sts. K 59 rows.

Next row (RS): K9, p1, k5, p1, k9.

Next row (WS): K4, p to last 4 sts, k4.

Rep last 2 rows 3 times more.

Next row: K15, p1, knit to end.

Next row: K4, purl to last 4 sts, k4.

Rep last 2 rows twice more.

Next row: Knit.

Next row: K4, purl to last 4 sts, k4.

Rep last 2 rows twice more.

Knit 6 rows.

BO, leaving a long tail for sewing seam.

Finishing

With yarn of choice, embroider lazy daisies (see page 15) to top of "stems."

Fold work in half lengthwise with RS facing. Join side seams, leaving top open and yarn tail untrimmed. Turn right side out, fill with herbs, and finish joining top seam. Attach ribbon to 2 adjacent outside corners of pillow with needle and thread.

Birdy Cardigan

Many vintage patterns use motifs to decorate finished pieces. I much prefer adding a design after the garment is knitted, so I can play with color and placement, removing the stitches easily if I change my mind. This everyday-use raglan cardigan with blue birds was inspired by a vintage pattern but uses a modern cashmere-blend yarn for softness and easy care.

Sizes

3–6 months (6–12 months, 1–2 years, 2–3 years)

Finished Measurements

Chest width (buttoned): 19" (21", 23", 25") (48.5 [53.5, 58.5, 63.5] cm)

Length from back neck: 10½" (12", 13½", 14¾") (26.5 [30.5, 34.5, 37.5] cm)

Sleeve seam: 6" (7½", 9", 10½") (15 [19, 23, 27] cm)

Materials

3 (4, 4, 5) 50 g balls Debbie Bliss Baby Cashmerino (55% merino wool, 33% microfiber, 12% cashmere; 137 yds [125 m]) in #202 Baby Blue

Yarn oddments for duplicate stitch embroidery (in the photo, Baby Cashmerino in #203 Teal)

US 3 (3.25 mm) straight needles

US 4 (3.5 mm) straight needles

Stitch holders

Safety pins to mark buttonholes

Removable row marker

Stitch marker

5 (¾" [2 cm]) buttons

Yarn needle for finishing

Needle and thread to match cardigan yarn

Gauge

25 sts and 34 rows make 4" (10 cm) on larger needles in St st

Directions

Back

On smaller needles, CO 59 (65, 71, 77) sts.

Row 1 (RS): *K1, p1; rep from * to last st, k1.

Rep Row 1, 5 (5, 7, 7) times more to create seed st edge.

Change to larger needles, and work in St st, beg with a knit row, until back measures 6" (7", 8", 9") (15 [18, 20, 23] cm) from CO edge, ending with a purl row.

Back Raglan Shaping

BO 4 sts at beg of next 2 rows—51 (57, 63, 69) sts.

Next row (RS): K1, sl1, k1, psso, k to last 3 sts, k2tog, k1—49 (55, 61, 67) sts.

Next row (WS): Purl.

Repeat these 2 rows until 19 (21, 23, 25) sts rem, ending with a purl row.

Sl sts onto a stitch holder.

Left Front

On smaller needles, CO 34 (37, 40, 43) sts.

✿ *3–6 months and 1–2 years:*

Row 1 (RS): *P1, k1; rep from * to end.

Row 2 (WS): *K1, p1; rep from * to end.

Rep Rows 1–2, 2 (3) times more.

✿ *6–12 months and 2–3 years:*

Row 1 (RS): *K1, p1; rep from * to last st, k1.

Rep this row 5 (7) times more.

✿ *All sizes:*

Change to larger needles.

Next row (RS): K to last 6 sts, seed st 6.

Next row (WS): Seed st 6, purl to end.

Rep last 2 rows until work measures same as back to armhole, ending on a WS row.

Left Front Raglan Shaping

BO 4 sts at beg of next row—30 (33, 36, 39) sts.

Next row (WS): Seed st 6, purl to end.

(continued)

Next row (RS): K1, sl1, k1, psso, k to last 6 sts, seed st 6.

Rep last 2 rows until 20 (21, 22, 23) sts rem, ending with a WS row.

Left Front Neck Shaping

Next row (RS): K1, sl1, k1, psso, k10, turn; sl rem 7 (8, 9, 10) sts onto a stitch holder—12 sts on needle.

Next row (WS): Purl.

Next row: K1, sl1, k1, psso, k to last 3 sts, sl1, k1, psso, k1—10 sts.

Rep last 2 rows until 4 sts rem, ending with a WS row.

Next row: K1, sl1, k2tog, psso, BO rem 2 sts purlwise.

Mark placement of 5 buttons with safety pins. Position top button on Row 4 of neckband, bottom button on Row 5 of seed st hem, middle 3 buttons evenly between.

Right Front

On smaller needles, CO 34 (37, 40, 43) sts.

❋ *3–6 months and 1–2 years:*

Row 1 (RS): *K1, p1; rep from * to end.

Row 2 (WS): *P1, k1; rep from * to end.

Rows 3–4: Rep Rows 1–2.

Row 5 (buttonhole): K1, p1, k1, yo, k2tog, p1, *k1, p1; rep from * to end.

Row 6: *P1, k1; rep from * to end.

Rep Rows 1–2, 0 (1) times more.

❋ *6–12 months and 2–3 years:*

Rows 1–4: *K1, p1; rep from * to last st, k1.

Row 5 (RS) (buttonhole): *K1, p1, k1, yo, k2tog, *p1, k1; rep from * to end.

Row 6 (WS): *K1, p1; rep from * to last st, k1.

Rep Row 6, 0 (2) times more.

❋ *All sizes:*

Change to larger needles.

Next row (RS): Seed st 6, knit to end.

Next row (WS): P to last 6 sts, seed st 6.

Rep last 2 rows and, *at the same time*, cont making buttonholes to match pin positions for button placement on left front, until work measures same as back to armhole, ending with a RS row.

Right Front Raglan Shaping

BO 4 sts at beg of next row.

Next row (RS): Seed st 6, k to last 3 sts, k2tog, k1.

Next row (WS): P to last 6 sts, seed st 6.

Rep the last 2 rows, making buttonholes at pin positions, until 19 (20, 21, 22) sts rem. End with a RS row.

Right Front Neck Shaping

Next row (WS): P12, turn, and sl rem 7 (8, 9, 10) sts onto stitch holder.

Next row (RS): K1, k2tog, k to last 3 sts, k2tog, k1—2 sts dec'd.

Next row: Purl.

Rep last 2 rows until 4 sts rem, ending with a WS row.

Next row: K3tog, k1.

BO rem 2 sts purlwise.

Sleeve (Make 2)

On smaller needles, CO 35 (37, 39, 41) sts.

Rows 1–8: *K1, p1; rep from * to last st, k1.

Change to larger needles, and work in St st for 4 rows, beg with a knit row.

Inc 1 st at each end of next row and every 8th row foll until you have 47 (51, 55, 59) sts.

Work even until sleeve measures 6" (7½", 9", 10½") (15 [19, 23, 27] cm) from beg, ending with a purl row. Place removable marker at end of last row.

Work even for 6 more rows (these 6 rows are set into armhole shaping and are not included in sleeve seam measurement).

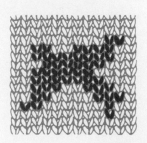

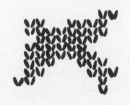

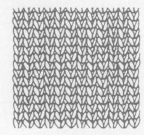

Sleeve Raglan Shaping

Next row (RS): K1, sl1, k1, psso, k to last 3 sts, k2tog, k1—2 sts dec'd.

Next row (WS): Purl.

Rep these 2 rows until 37 sts rem, ending with a purl row.

Next row: K1, sl1, k1, psso, k13, sl1, k1, psso, k1, place stitch marker for center of row, k2tog, k13, k2tog, k1—33 sts.

Cont to dec 1 st at each end of every RS row as before and, *at the same time*, dec 2 sts in center of every 6th row 3 times more, until 7 sts rem, ending with a purl row. Sl sts onto a stitch holder.

Neckband

Join raglan seams, sewing last 6 rows of sleeve seam to the 4 BO sts at armholes.

On smaller needles with RS facing, sl the 7 (8, 9, 10) sts of right front neck from stitch holder onto needle, join yarn, pick up evenly and k9 sts along side of front neck, k across sts of right sleeve, back neck, and left sleeve, as you k2tog at each seamline; pick up evenly and k9 sts along left front neck, then work in pattern across the 7 (8, 9, 10) sts from left front neck stitch holder—63 (67, 71, 75) sts.

Work 7 rows in seed st, making buttonhole as on Row 4.

BO in seed stitch, knitting together every 7th and 8th sts.

Finishing

Press pieces with a warm iron and a damp cloth. Join side and sleeve seems. Sew on buttons. Weave in ends. Add bird motif using duplicate stitch (see page 13).

Hooded Capelet

Inspired by *Little Red Riding Hood*, this fun little cape sports an adorable vintage peaked hood and fluffy pom-poms. Super-soft cashmere-merino yarn keeps head and shoulders warm, while busy hands are free to carry a basket of goodies to grandmother's house.

Sizes

6–12 months (1–2, 2–3 years)

Finished Measurements

Length at back center: 10" (12", 14") (25 [31, 36] cm)

Materials

3 (4, 5) 50 g balls RYC Cashsoft Baby DK (57% extra-fine merino, 33% microfiber, 10% cashmere; 143 yds [130 m]), in #801 Horseradish

US 6 (4 mm) 24" (60 cm) circular needle

Yarn needle for finishing

2 (3, 3) (½" [13 mm]) buttons

Needle and thread to match yarn

Gauge

22 sts and 28 rows make 4" (10 cm) in St st

Directions

Base and Sides

CO 171 (175, 179) sts.

Rows 1–10: *K1, p1; rep from * to last st, k1.

Row 11 (RS): Work 8 sts in seed st pattern, k to last 8 sts, seed st 8.

Row 12 (WS): Seed st 8, p to last 8 sts, seed st 8.

Rep Rows 11–12 until work measures 7½" (9½", 11½") (19 [24, 29] cm), ending with a WS row.

Top Shaping

Row 1 (RS) (buttonhole): Seed st 3, yo, k2tog, seed st 3, k3, *k2, k2tog; repeat from * to last 8 sts, seed st 8—133 (136, 139) sts.

Row 2 and all WS rows: Seed st 8, p to last 8 sts, seed st 8.

Row 3: Seed st 8, k to last 8 sts, seed st 8.

Row 5: Seed st 8, k1 (0, 3) sts, *k2, k2tog; repeat from * to last 8 sts, seed st 8—104 (106, 109) sts.

Row 7: Seed st 8, k to last 8 sts, seed st 8.

Row 9: Seed st 8, k0 (2, 3) sts, *k2 (2, 3) sts, k2tog; repeat from * to last 8 sts, seed st 8—82 (84, 91) sts.

Row 11 (buttonhole): Seed st 3, yo, k2tog, seed st 3, k to last 8 sts, seed st 8.

Row 13: Seed st 8, k2 (3, 0) sts, *k2 (3, 3) sts, k2tog; rep from * to last 8 sts, seed st 8—66 (71, 76) sts.

Row 15: Seed st 8, k to last 8 sts, seed st 8.

Row 17: Seed st 8, *k3, k2tog; rep from * to last 8 sts, seed st 8—56 (60, 64) sts.

Row 19 (eyelet row): Seed st 8, *k3, yo, k2tog; repeat from * to last 8 (12, 11) sts, k0 (4, 3) sts, seed st 8.

Row 20: Seed st 8, p to last 8 sts, seed st 8.

BO in seed stitch.

(continued)

Hood

CO 42 (48, 52) sts.

Row 1 (RS): Seed st 12, knit to end.

Row 2 (WS): P to last 12 sts, seed st to end.

Rep Rows 1–2 until work measures 1" (1½", 1½") (2 [3, 3] cm).

Next row: To shape back, inc 1 st at St st edge (back edge). Inc 1 st at same edge every 1" (2.5 cm) foll 6 more times—49 (55, 59) sts.

Work even for 1" (1½", 2") (3 [4, 6] cm).

Next row: Dec 1 st at back edge. Dec 1 at same edge every 1" (2.5 cm) foll 6 more times—42 (48, 52) sts.

Work even for 1" (1½", 1½") (2 [3, 3] cm).

Work should measure 15" (16", 16½") (38 [40, 42] cm) from beg.

BO loosely.

Finishing

With a slightly damp cloth and a warm iron, press lightly on WS. Fold hood in half lengthwise with RS together, and join center back seam. Fold 6 sts of seed st border to RS, and secure as you sew hood to BO edge of capelet neck, using a flat seam and easing hood to fit between seed st borders of capelet. Sew on buttons. Weave in ends.

With yarn, make twisted cord 22" (56 cm) long (see page 14). Thread cord through eyelets. Make 2 pom-poms (see page 14), and attach them to ends of twisted cord.

Resources

Knitting Websites

Knitting Help
www.knittinghelp.com
A very helpful site full of clear videos on common stitch techniques and knitting how-tos.

Ravelry
www.ravelry.com
A knit and crochet social networking site that lets you share and rate patterns, yarns, books, and materials. A great place to find new ideas.

Yarn Manufacturers

Blue Sky Alpacas
www.blueskyalpacas.com

Debbie Bliss
www.debbieblissonline.com

Jo Sharp
www.josharp.com.au

Sublime Yarns
www.sublimeyarns.com

Rowan
www.knitrowan.com

Suppliers in New Zealand

Knit World
www.knitting.co.nz
Stocks Jo Sharp, Sublime, Rowan, RYC

Nancy's Embroidery
www.nancys.co.nz
Stocks Debbie Bliss

South Seas Knitting
www.southseasknitting.com
Stocks Blue Sky Alpacas

Suppliers in Australia

The Wool Shack
www.thewoolshack.com
Stocks Sublime, Debbie Bliss, Jo Sharp, Blue Sky Alpacas

Suppliers in United Kingdom

Angel Yarns
www.angelyarns.com
Stocks Debbie Bliss, Rowan, RYC, Sublime

Loop Yarn

www.loopyarn.com

Stocks Sublime, Debbie Bliss, Blue Sky Alpacas

International Suppliers

Jimmy Beans Wool

www.jimmybeanswool.com

Purl Soho

www.purlsoho.com

Yarn Market

www.yarnmarket.com

Suggested Reading

Some of the books that have inspired me are these:

Baby Knits for Beginners, Debbie Bliss
(North Pomfret, VT: Trafalgar Square, 2003)
A wonderful book for the beginner who wants to
create simple baby clothes while learning to knit.

Knitting for Baby, Melanie Falick and Kristin Nicholas (New York: Stewart, Tabori & Chang, 2002)
A learn-to-knit book filled with easy patterns and
great hand-holding advice.

Last-Minute Knitted Gifts, Joelle Hoverson
(New York: Stewart, Tabori & Chang, 2004)
Filled with beautiful little projects, including a
few baby items, that you can knit in less than four
hours; from my favorite knitting shop, Purl Soho
(purlsoho.com).

Simple Knits for Cherished Babies, Erika Knight
(London: Collins & Brown, 2005)
A gorgeous book of baby knits from one of the best
knitwear designers in the UK.

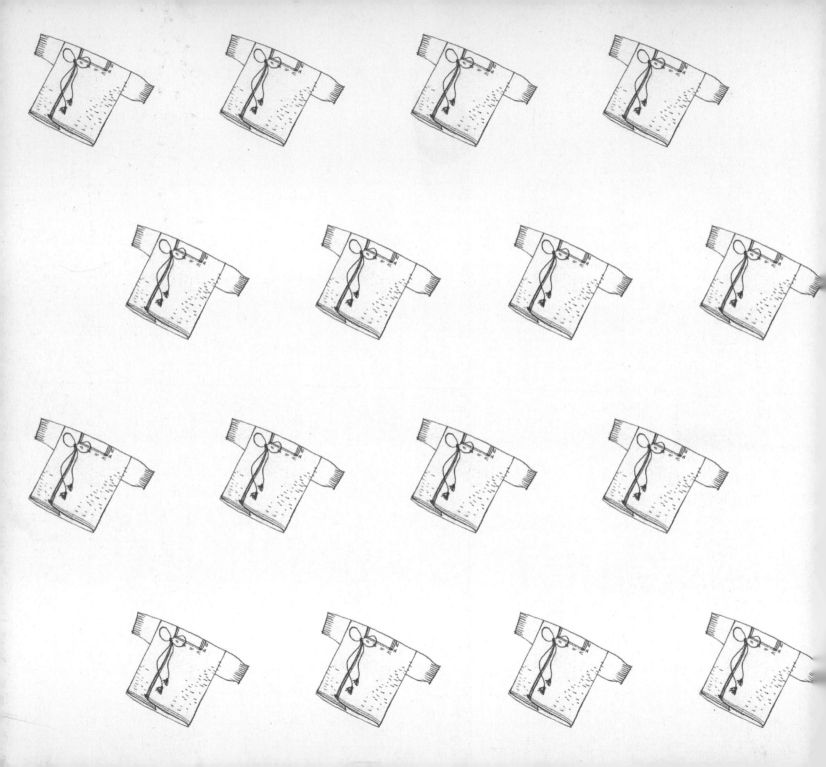